INTERPRETING
PAUL'S GOSPEL

INTERPRETING
PAUL'S GOSPEL

by

A. M. HUNTER

SCM PRESS LTD
56 BLOOMSBURY STREET
LONDON

First published 1954
Second impression 1955
Third impression 1960
Fourth impression 1962

*Printed in Great Britain by Offset Lithography
by Billing and Sons, Ltd. Guildford and London*

CONTENTS

Preface   9

Part One

THE GOSPEL ACCORDING
TO ST. PAUL

INTRODUCTION   13

I. THE BACKGROUND   17

II. SALVATION AS A PAST EVENT   21

III. SALVATION AS A PRESENT EXPERIENCE   36

IV. SALVATION AS A FUTURE HOPE   50

V. THE SAVIOUR   56

Part Two

THE GOSPEL ACCORDING TO
ST. PAUL FOR TODAY

I. OUR HUMAN PREDICAMENT   67

     1. *St. Paul's Doctrine of Sin*   68
         A state of radical wrongness infecting every man and
         exposing him to the divine condemnation.
         The "Fall" and "the Wrath of God".

     2. *Is Paul's diagnosis true and tenable today?*   71
         The discrediting of modern views of evil and a return
         to more biblical insights.
         The case of C. E. M. Joad.

     3. *The Dimension of the Demonic*   74
         Paul and the "powers" of darkness.
         Revival of belief in the demonic.

4. *Modern Man and Original Sin*   76

Modern man does not see sin as sin because he has lost his awareness of the living God.

The need to proclaim both God and his forgiveness.

Note on "the Wrath of God"

II. The Way of Deliverance   81

1. *The Way of Deliverance in Paul's Gospel*   81

God's deed in the Cross of Christ, bringing a new start and status for the sinner.

2. *Is the Way out of date?*   82

Christ the eternal Contemporary.

Legalism is not dead.

What is needed for understanding Paul's Gospel is "despair".

The testimony of the saints to its truth.

3. *The Communication of the Gospel*   85

How shall we preach "justification" to modern man?

Reconciliation (as expounded in "the Prodigal Son") is the needed category.

4. *The Preaching of the Cross*   88

Its difficulties today.

The abiding magnetism of "the Strange Man on his Cross".

Theories of the Atonement: revelatory, dramatic and penal.

The enduring obligation to preach "Christ crucified".

III. Newness of Life: (1) Fellowship with Christ   94

Salvation as a present experience: "newness of life".

The "old man" and the "new man".

1. *Life "in communion with Christ"*   95

is of the essence of Paul's Christianity and should be fundamental today.

Contents

2. *Life "in the community of Christ"*   99
The Church is central to Paul's Gospel.
What Paul can teach us about:
    the nature of the Church;
    the unity of the Church;
    the mission of the Church.

3. *Life in koinōnia*   104
Paul's conception of Baptism and the Eucharist.
Real sacraments mediating communion with the living Crucified.
The threefold aspect of the Eucharist.

IV. NEWNESS OF LIFE: (2) POWER AND PRINCIPLES   107

  1. *The Power of the New Life: the Holy Spirit*   107
The richness of Paul's doctrine of the Spirit.
The evident loss of spiritual power today.
Modern vagueness about the Spirit, and its causes.
Whatever is not apostolic is not safe.

  2. *The Principles of the New Life*   114
    (*a*) Paul's theory of the good life:
        "Grace" goodness;
        "Live and do this."
    (*b*) Elementary ethics for "babes" in Christ.
    (*c*) Paul's pattern for the good life, its motives and principles.
        Noblesse oblige—the *koinōnia* motive—*Lex Christi*
        —*Agapē*

V. THE HOPE OF GLORY   121
Paul's eschatological certitudes.
The revolt from traditional eschatology.
The need for new thinking about the Last Things.
We must take Paul's views seriously, if not literally.

  1. *The Beginning of the End—"D-Day is past"*   125
Is the authentic Easter note missing from our worship?

Contents

The apostolic conviction of the regnant Christ, and its relevance.

2. *The Hope of the Day of Christ*   127
"D-Day" and "V-Day".
How should we think about the Second Advent?
We must believe in a real End when what is valuable in human history will be taken up into eternity.
Our clue to the Second Coming is the First.

3. *The Years of Grace*   130
Modern scepticism about the idea of progress.
St. Paul's conception of the purpose of the years of grace.
The need to recover a true Christian optimism about the future of earthly history.

4. *The Heart of the Christian Hope*   133
   (*a*) Immortality is a gift of God.
   (*b*) Its mode is a new body.
   (*c*) It means an existence at once corporate and Christ-like.

INDEX   141

PREFACE

The second part of this book contains five of the seven James Sprunt Lectures which I gave in Union Theological Seminary, Richmond, Virginia, in the first week of March, 1954. To the Trustees of the Lectureship who honoured me with the invitation to Richmond, I should like to give thanks, as I express my deep gratitude to President Lacy and his colleagues on the Faculty at Richmond who showed me uncommon kindness during my few days there.

In order to make a book out of the lectures, I have printed in Part I a short sketch of Paul's theology (the substance of which, much abbreviated, formed my first two Sprunt Lectures). This, besides providing a basis for Part II, may be of some help to theological students.

To unlock the wards of Paul's theology, I have unashamedly borrowed the key (the word "salvation") which Anderson Scott, a quarter of a century ago, so successfully employed in his *Christianity according to St Paul*, in many ways still the best book on Paul's theology we have.

Part II endeavours to show that the Gospel expounded in Part I is still relevant in the middle of this twentieth century.

The renderings of New Testament passages are normally those of the American Revised Standard Version of the Bible copyrighted 1946 and 1952 by permission of Thomas Nelson & Sons Ltd., Edinburgh, and, in U.S.A., of the Division of Christian Education of the National Council of Churches. I am indebted to the editors of *Interpretation* for permission to reprint Chapter V in Part Two.

Two Aberdeen colleagues deserve my thanks: Professor David Cairns, who read the typescript; and Dr John Gray, who helped me with the proofs.

King's College   A. M. H.
  Aberdeen University
  May 1954

9

Part One

THE GOSPEL ACCORDING
TO ST. PAUL

INTRODUCTION

The Gospel of Christ, as St. Paul understood it, is the Good
News of the salvation which God has provided through
Christ's incarnation, death, resurrection and living power,
and now offers to all men who will believe. What we call his
theology is that Gospel as explicated in his letters. "St. Paul's
theology is not something which anybody can separate
from his Gospel; it is his Gospel itself as his mind grasped
it."[1]

Why should we study it? The short answer is, "Because
St. Paul was the first, and probably the greatest, of the
interpreters of the Fact of Christ. Better than any other he
divined what Christ was, and is."

But not all have given this answer. Not a few down the
centuries have shown some disposition to agree with the
Pardoner in Sir David Lindsay's *Three Estates*:

> *By him that bore the crown of thorn,*
> *I would St. Paul had never been born.*

And some have bluntly pronounced St. Paul's theology to
be a disastrous mistake. Less than a hundred years ago,
Renan, prophesying that the day of "the ugly little Jew"
was over, made bold to say: "The writings of Paul have
been a peril and a stumbling-block, the cause of the principal
defects of Christian theology." Many another, less famous
than Renan, has deemed Paul "the villain of the piece"—
the arch-corrupter who turned an originally simple Gospel
of God's fatherhood and man's brotherhood into an

[1] Denney, *Expositor*, Jan. 1901, 4.

elaborate cosmic drama of redemption. But Paul has suffered hardly less at the hands of his too-zealous friends, those expounders of Paulinism who almost smothered his Gospel beneath their learned treatises on Hamartiology, Soteriology, Pneumatology and the rest.

Yet Paul's Christianity has never died; on the contrary, in past centuries it has shown an astonishing power to quicken and revitalize the Christian religion when it seemed fallen upon evil days; and one after another, the great seminal thinkers of the Church—Augustine, Luther, Calvin, Wesley and Barth—have risen up to name Paul master in their trade, persuaded that he better than any other of the apostolic men had grasped "the truth as it is in Jesus".

Some may grant all this, and still feel that, after all is said, Paul remains a man of his time whose theology has very little bearing on our time and our problems. To all such Karl Barth makes this reply[1]:

"Paul, as a child of his time, addressed his contemporaries. As prophet and apostle of the Kingdom of God, he veritably speaks to all men of every age. . . . If we rightly understand ourselves, our problems are the problems of Paul, and if we be enlightened by the brightness of his answers, those answers must be our answers too."

This is the conviction in which this book is written. To be sure, Paul's thought often requires translation into terms appropriate to the middle of the twentieth century, if it is to come home to us and grip us. Sometimes his arguments will make us sympathize with Martin Luther when he lighted upon a piece of rabbinical exegesis in Paul's letters: "Brother Paul, this does not hold." On some points, indeed, we may feel obliged to dissent rather sharply from him. For an example: "I had been reading the ninth chapter of Romans,"

[1] *Romans*, E.T., 1.

writes Principal Cairns in his autobiography,[1] "and when I came upon the passage about 'vessels of wrath' and 'Who art thou O man, that repliest against God?' my mind gave a mental spring, and said in effect, 'I do!' This is an unjust and tyrannous endeavour to override conscience, and it *cannot* be God."

Nevertheless, to dismiss Paul's theology as "obsolete stuff" because we disagree with this or that point of detail, or because we dislike Paul's gloomy view of man apart from Christ, or because we judge his opinions on Christian marriage to be very defective, would be a profound mistake. Real and permanent issues underlie the temporary problems Paul discusses, e.g. the controversy about salvation by faith or by works. And if we grant what we may call Paul's major premiss (which as Christians we can hardly help doing) that there is a living God outside the world-process, who shapes the course of history and once broke openly and decisively into it in the Man called Jesus of Nazareth, then the main lines of his theology stand firm, and we no less than his first converts may make that theology our own.

> *Long, long ago the Truth was found.*
> *A company of men it bound.*
> *Grasp firmly then—that ancient Truth.*"[2]

---

[1] *David Cairns, An Autobiography*, 121.
[2] Quoted Barth, *Romans*, E.T., 1.

Chapter One

THE BACKGROUND[1]

St. Paul was a Jew, living mostly in a Gentile environment, who had become a Christian. The background of his theology is therefore threefold: Jewish, Greek and Christian.

His debt to Judaism is writ so large in every letter that it hardly needs to be elaborated. "The Hebrew son of Hebrew parents" (Phil. 3.5), he was nurtured in the *Credo* of Pharisaism, which may be summed up as belief in the one righteous and holy God, in the law (or *Torah*) as the unique revelation of God's will for man and in the election of Israel as his special People. These things are basic to Paul's thought; and though his conversion cut his life in two and made "a new creature" of him, he remained to the end a Jew, proud of his race, conscious of his high privileges, deep-versed in his people's scriptures and—though called to be the Apostle to the Gentiles—looking for the salvation of the world in terms of the salvation of God's own People —"and so all Israel shall be saved" (Rom. 11.26).

Gilbert Murray[2] has called Paul "one of the great figures of Greek literature". What did he owe to Hellenism? He read his scriptures in a Greek translation—the Septuagint. He wrote his letters in the *Koiné*, or "Common Greek", which was the *lingua franca* of the age. He spent most of his thirty years as a Christian in lands where Greek culture,

---

[1] We take all the epistles commonly ascribed to Paul to be genuine, except the Pastorals.　　[2] *Four Stages of Greek Religion*, 146.

civilization and religion met him at every turn. We may not deny the influence of all this upon him. Twice or thrice he quotes Greek poets; he borrows illustrations from the Greek games (running, boxing, wrestling, the arena) and from Graeco-Roman processes of law (e.g. "adoption"); here and there he employs a Stoic word like "conscience" or a Stoic idea, like that of "the law written on the heart" (Rom. 2.14f.); and sometimes words used by devotees of the Greek Mystery Religions ("mystery", "initiated", etc.) fall from his pen. But the notion of strong Stoic influence on his thought is not to be taken seriously, and the theory, once fashionable in Germany, that his thinking about the sacraments was deeply infected by the Mysteries has lost caste in the world of scholarship. If we may not deny Paul's debt to Hellenism, we must not overrate it. It was superficial, not fundamental. The idiom of his thought is Hebrew; his great keywords ("righteousness", "faith", etc.) have their roots deep in the Old Testament; his dialectic is often rabbinical; and his conceptions of God and man and time and eternity owe far more to Jewish than to Greek sources. John Oman once observed: "The stronger a man's natural quality, the more likely it is to remain racy of his native soil." Though the surface of Paul's thought may owe much to Hellenism, its sub-soil remained Jewish.[1]

Now consider his Christian debt. People who talk vaguely about "Paulinism" often forget that Paul owed a great deal to his Christian predecessors. Sometimes, as in I Cor. 15.3ff., he tells us expressly that he is repeating something he himself had "received" from them. But much else in his letters is the common apostolic Christianity which existed before Paul wrote a single letter. His *kerygma* (or "preached message") was the common apostolic Gospel. "Whether then

[1] See W. D. Davies: *St. Paul and Rabbinic Judaism*, 321.

it be I or they [Peter, James and the rest]," he says, "so we preach and so you believed" (I Cor. 15.11). The "words of the Lord" to which he refers (I Cor. 7.10, 9.14, Acts 20.35) came to him through his Christian predecessors. Paul was not the first to invest Christ's death with atoning significance. He did not invent the two sacraments of baptism and the Lord's Supper, any more than he created the doctrine of the Holy Spirit. If Paul worshipped Jesus as Messiah and Lord, so did those who were Christians before him. One of the greatest passages in his letters about Christ—Phil. 2.6–11— may well be a pre-Pauline Christian hymn.[1] In short, we err if we picture Paul as a spiritual Columbus "voyaging through strange seas of thought alone". Original Paul was, and his own deep religious experience undoubtedly counted for much; but the thing about which he writes with such creative power was the common Christian faith which stemmed from those who were "in Christ" before him.

Our spiritual prolegomena to Paul have still to mention one fact of palmary importance—his conversion.

Somebody has said Paul's faith bears not so much the grammarian's as the sinner's touch. It is the theology of a converted man, of one who could say, "By the grace of God I am what I am" (I Cor. 15.10). No doubt it took time for all the implications of the Damascus Road experience to become clear to him; but we may safely say that for Paul it brought four decisive consequences. To begin with, it meant that Christ was incontrovertibly alive—alive by the power of God, who through the Resurrection had set his seal on the work of the Cross. Second, the Cross itself, which had been for Paul the persecutor the sign of God's curse (Gal. 3.13), became for him the supreme proof of God's love (Rom. 5.8). Third, Paul knew now that "salvation is of the Lord"—

[1] So Lohmeyer, Hering, Cullmann, Jeremias, etc.

that it begins on the divine side with an act of pure grace which man has done nothing to deserve. For, when he was still a sinner, God had reconciled him to himself. And finally, in the high hour of his conversion, Paul saw not only the living Christ but "the vision of a waiting world" and of himself as God's *apostolos*—his chosen envoy—to it.

All these convictions, born of his encounter with Christ on the Damascus Road, were to colour deeply his later thinking and theology.

Chapter Two

SALVATION AS A
PAST EVENT

We are ready now to study St. Paul's Christianity. But the question arises: Is there any keyword or concept which will lead us, as with an Ariadne's thread, to the heart of it, and enable us to see it as a whole?

The answer of traditional Protestantism has been: "Justification by faith". So Luther judged, and in his hand the doctrine

> *became a trumpet, whence he blew*
> *Soul-animating strains.*

But "justification by faith", as we shall see, is but the fragment of a bigger whole, or, if you like, the first step on the journey, not the whole road. Others have suggested: "union with Christ". "The religion of Paul", said Deissmann,[1] "is quite simple. It is communion with Christ." Again we must pronounce this only an element, though, to be sure, a very important one, in Paul's Christianity. The word we need must be more comprehensive.

"The fundamental question of religion", it has been said, "is, What must I do to be saved? Paul's theology starts from this question."[2] So, when he preaches at Pisidian Antioch, or writes to the Christians in Rome, it is this word

---

[1] *The Religion of Jesus and the Faith of Paul*, 223.
[2] Weinel, *Paul, the Man and His Work*, 289.

"salvation" which he uses. "To us is the word of this salvation sent forth" (Acts 13.26). "The Gospel is the power of God unto salvation" (Rom. 1.16).[1]

"Salvation" is the word we need. Greek and Jew in Paul's day would probably have disagreed about what they wished to be saved from: for the Greek, it would be from fate and the fear of annihilation; for the Jew, it would be pre-eminently from the sin which separates from a holy God. But salvation was that for which both yearned, and in the Gospel Paul claimed he had what they sought. Nor, in his view, was the Gospel simply something negative—safety from the long-term consequences of sin—a mere remedial system. It included not only what men must be saved *from*—sin and the flesh and death—but also what they must be saved *to*—reconciliation and righteousness and life.

Now, in the New Testament, as Lightfoot said, "salvation is a thing of the past, a thing of the present, and a thing of the future". This is true of St. Paul. "We were saved", he says (Rom. 8.24). "We are being saved" (I Cor. 15.2). "We shall be saved" (Rom. 5.9). Indeed, his whole doctrine of salvation is contained in Rom. 5.1: "Therefore being justified by faith, we have peace with God through our Lord Jesus Christ; through whom also we have access by faith into this grace wherein we stand, and rejoice in hope of the glory of God."

As Paul thinks of salvation, he looks back to the time when, by faith, the believer received God's forgiveness in Christ; he dwells on his present blessedness ("this grace wherein we stand"), and he looks forward to the time when, with sin and death no more, he will enjoy the Beatific Vision.

[1] *cf.* Eph. 1.13 "the gospel of your salvation".

Our exposition of Paul's theology will be simply an expansion of this pregnant verse in Romans.

Salvation as a Past Event

Salvation, as a thing of the past, looks back to the finished work of Christ on the Cross and the believer's sharing in its virtue.

Paul thinks of it in terms of three picture-phrases: as redemption, as justification and as reconciliation. The first pictures an enslaved man being set free; the second, a guilty man being acquitted; and the third, an estranged child being taken back into his parent's favour.

"Redemption" (*apolytrōsis*: Rom. 3.24, Col. 1.14; *cf.* also Paul's use of the verbs "redeem" and "set free" in passages like Gal. 3.13; 4.5, Rom. 6.18; 8.2) signified originally the liberation of a slave or a prisoner by payment of a price. Acquiring the more general meaning of "deliverance", it had been used in the Septuagint to describe God's deliverance of his People from their Egyptian bondage. Paul uses it to express the deliverance of Christians from the bondage of sin. Christ, he says, has delivered us from our thraldom of sin, which brings in its train death.

So let us pause to examine his doctrine not only of sin but of "the flesh" and "the law" which together make up a terrible triumvirate from which man needs to be delivered.

Generally Paul talks of sin, not sins. But what he has to say about it is profoundly experimental. He tells the truth about sin as in his experience he has come to know it. Though he never formally defines it, he sees it in relation to the law of God—as a violation of the commandments in which that law is set forth. "Without the law, I should not have known sin", he says. As a Jew he naturally thinks of the law of Moses, but not of it only. It is but the clearest

23

expression of a universal and eternal law of God in some degree known and accessible to all, Gentiles as well as Jews.

Sin, then, is "a going wrong"; but Paul's is no "atomic" theory of sin. Unlike the moralist, he does not regard it merely as a series of wrong choices or moral mis-steps which a man may stop if he has a mind to. It is a positive and destructive principle endemic in man. More, it is a social, corporate wrongness—a state of the race in which things have gone radically awry.

As to its origin, in one passage (Rom. 5.12ff.) he traces the sin of all men to Adam's primeval act of disobedience which

Brought death into the world, and all our woe.

Elsewhere, as in Rom. 1.18–32, he seems to find its root in man's turning away from the true knowledge of God revealed to him. As to its nature, he regards it as an evil power, indwelling and enslaving man, so that, to get Paul's full meaning, we have almost to spell it with a capital S. As to its range, Paul regards it as universal: "all have sinned". As to its effect, it brings man under God's condemnation and wrath. And as to its cure, the only remedy lies in "the redemption which is in Christ Jesus". Only by faith in the living Christ who has died for our sins, can we find deliverance from the curse and condemnation of sin.

The tool which sin uses is the *flesh (Sarx)*, which is not the same thing as the body. Basically, the flesh is the material side of man's nature, not necessarily evil. But since sin, using the flesh as its "base of operations", has corrupted it, it is no longer morally neutral. It has become the involuntary accomplice of sin, who is the real criminal. As the material which gives sin its chance, it comes to signify not merely man in his natural weakness (as often in the Old

Testament) but man as fallen—human nature as apostate from God.

Thus, to "trust in the flesh" or "walk by the flesh" is not so much to give way to the lower passions—though that is involved—as to live Godlessly, in sinful self-reliance. It means to turn away from the Creator and to find one's security in the creation, which is transient and perishable. The opposite of this is to live "by the Spirit"; and as the Spirit produces life and peace, so the flesh brings ruin and death (Rom. 8.6ff.). In Barth's words[1], the flesh stands for "the complete inadequacy of the creature before his Creator", for which the sole cure is "the Spirit of life which is in Christ Jesus" (Rom. 8.2).

The third member in the triumvirate is the law—primarily the law of Moses, but that law as an expression of the universal law of God.

Paul speaks of "the curse of the law" (Gal. 3.13). Yet elsewhere he can call it "holy" and say it was meant "to give life" (Rom. 7.10, 12). How can the law be described in one place as the holy demand of God and in another as a slavery driving a man to despair? The explanation is that it is not the law (which, so far as it contains the moral demands of God, is still valid) but "legalism" which is the curse. Legalism is the attempt to "live"—to find salvation—under the law, by obeying its statutes, and so obtaining credit in the ledgers of heaven. It is believing you can do and be good in your own strength. The "legal" man is the religiously "self-made man". But as Paul found, and countless others have found since, not that way lies salvation. No man can earn God's favour by works of law. Let mortal man present himself before the Most High clad in his works of law, and the verdict must ever be: "Unrighteous!"

[1] *Romans*, E.T., 89.

So Paul came to a clear conclusion. The law is powerless to save—powerless because it is weak through the flesh (Rom. 8.3). He came to another—one which we too can verify for ourselves: the law produces a sense of sin, even provokes to sinning (Rom. 3.20; 7.7, I Cor. 15.56) (as the command "Thou shalt not steal" drove the youthful Augustine to raid a neighbour's orchard). So, thirdly, Paul came to see the purpose of the law as preparatory. It is a temporary expedient in God's plan (Rom. 5.20, Gal. 3.17), or, more positively, a *paidagōgos*—a "guardian" or "attendant"—designed to lead men to Christ's school (Gal. 3.24). For, with the coming of Christ, the day of law as a way of salvation is over (Rom. 10.4). In Christ there becomes possible a new relationship—that of sonship to God—one in which God's law is written on man's heart, in which love constrains to its doing and in which the Spirit is the power by which it is done. "Now discharged from the law," Paul says, "we serve not under the old written code but in the new life of the Spirit" (Rom. 7.6).

Paul's second term for salvation as a past event is "justification"—justification by grace through faith. The Greek noun is *dikaiōsis*; the verb *dikaioō*, which means not "make righteous" but "declare righteous" or "set right".

Justification means getting into right relations with God. How is a sinner to do this? Can he put himself right—say, by doing good works and so establishing a claim on God's favour? We know Paul's answer. No man can put himself right with God. Only God can do this. Justification is "the gracious action of God in accepting men as righteous in consequence of faith resting upon his redemptive activity in Christ".[1]

To understand Paul, we must first study his key-phrase

[1] V. Taylor, *Forgiveness and Reconciliation*, 57.

"the righteousness of God". This, as Paul uses it in passages like Rom 1.17 and 3.21, is not so much an attribute as an *activity* of God, with its clue in Old Testament usage, especially the Psalms and Part II of Isaiah. There the Hebrew *tsedaqah* rendered in the Septuagint by *dikaiosynē* means God's grace in action for the vindication of his People, "God putting things right" for them. It is a synonym for "salvation"—the activity in which God saves his People by rescuing them from their oppressors and delivering them from their sin. This is the meaning in such passages as:

"For my salvation is near to come
And my righteousness to be revealed" (Isa. 56.1).

"The Lord hath made known his salvation
His righteousness hath he openly shown in the sight
of the nations" (Ps. 98.2).

For such divine vindication—for a day when God would decisively redress all wrong and put things right—prophet and psalmist yearned in the centuries before Christ's coming. It was the heart of the Messianic hope.

With this background, we may now understand Paul when he says that the Gospel is the Good News that "the righteousness of God has been revealed". He is thinking of the divine activity by which God saves men in Christ and his Cross. It is his way of saying that in the life, death and resurrection of Christ the Kingdom of God has come.

The question, then, How is a sinner to get right with God? becomes, How is he to make this divine righteousness his own? And the answer is: By faith in Christ, whom God has made "our righteousness". When a sinful man commits himself in faith to Christ, who died for our sins, God of his grace justifies him—declares him righteous, puts him right with himself. This means not only pardon for his sins but the gift of a new standing with God.

This does not make him at once sinless. "The knight has been dubbed knight," says Brunner,[1] "but he is still in his condition a commoner; his nobility has not yet permeated his whole nature." But the justified man is potentially righteous: in virtue of his faith resting on the work of Christ, he is righteous in mind and purpose, if not yet in achievement; and he is called to become all that he is in germ.

"God", Paul says, "justifies the ungodly." There is paradox here. It suggests that God is a judge who acquits guilty men. But through his forensic language we get a glimpse of the amazing grace of God, and, at bottom, he is proclaiming the same saving truth as Jesus declared in the parable of the Prodigal Son. There, in the language not of the law-court but of the home, we see God, in a figure, "justifying the ungodly". The father's kiss, it has been said, is justification (as the ring and the robe are glorification). And justification is the first and decisive step on the road to salvation.

Paul's third term for salvation as a past event is "reconciliation". The Greek noun is *katallagē*, the verb *katallassō*, and the chief passages are Rom. 5.10f., II Cor. 5.18–20, Eph 2.16 and Col. 1.20f. And the basic idea is of restoration to fellowship with God.

This, we may well judge, is Paul's best way of putting it, because it lifts the whole issue from the level of the law-court to the plane of personal relations; because, too, the hunger for reconciliation with reality—however it be conceived—is something elemental and universal.

It is sin which creates the need for reconciliation. Sin destroys that fellowship with God for which man was made and which is his highest felicity. It sets up an estranging

[1] *Man in Revolt*, 491.

barrier between the holy God and sinful man, his creature. It interrupts the family relationship. Paul's name for this state is "alienation" (Eph. 4.18) or "hostility" (Col. 1.21).[1] Man's need is to recover the lost fellowship, to be restored to the family circle, to get out of dis-grace into grace. But he cannot do that for himself. Only God can do it. And, says Paul, it is the very heart of the Gospel that God has done it—in Christ crucified:

"God was in Christ reconciling the world to himself" (II Cor. 5.19).

"For if while we were enemies, we were reconciled to God by the death of his Son, much more, now that we are reconciled, shall we be saved by his life." (Rom 5.10), *cf.* Col. 1.20 and Eph 2.14–16.

We need only add that for Paul, as for all the New Testament writers, when reconciliation is in question, God is always the subject, as the object always is man. Paul never speaks of God being reconciled. No doubt, when men accept the reconciliation, and the estranging barrier falls away, a new situation arises for God as well as for man; but that is quite another thing from saying that God is reconciled.

The means of reconciliation is "the death of his Son", so that, as always in St. Paul, we are back at the Cross. To ask how the Cross effects reconciliation is to ask, What is Paul's doctrine of the Atonement?

This is too great a question to be adequately answered in a paragraph or two; but we may try to take the salient points. The first is that St. Paul did not invent the doctrine.

[1] There has been a long and indecisive debate about the meaning of *echthroi* in Rom. 5.10 and 11.28. Does it mean "hostile"? Or does Paul mean that sinners are the objects of divine hostility? Perhaps he means both.

That "Christ died for our sins"—that the forgiveness of
sins for the Christian is mediated through the death of
Christ—was part of what Paul had "received" from his
Christian predecessors (I Cor. 15.3), and for Paul, as for all
the apostolic men, the Cross was "the hiding-place of God's
power and inspiration of all Christian praise".

Yet so variously does he write of it that it is foolish to
try to confine his doctrine in a single formula. Here, if
anywhere, his phrase about "the many-splendoured wisdom
of God" (Eph. 3.10) has truth. Now he sees the Cross as the
supreme proof of the divine love: "God shows his love for
us in that while we were yet sinners Christ died for us"
(Rom. 5.8. How axiomatic it is for Paul that Christ's deed
of love on the Cross is God's deed! Said the boy Bevis, in
the story, as he looked at the picture of the Crucifixion: "If
God had been there, he wouldn't have let them do it." If
Paul is sure of anything, it is that God *was* there). Now he
sees the Cross as a spoiling of the principalities and powers
—a victory over the demonic powers of evil (Col. 2.15).
And now he sees it as a sacrifice for sin (Rom. 8.3).

But if we would penetrate more deeply into Paul's thought
about the death of Christ, there are three *loci classici*—one
in Romans, the second in II Corinthians and the third in
Galatians—to be studied.

The first, Rom. 3.24ff., is difficult. "They are justified by
his grace as a gift, through the redemption which is in
Christ Jesus, whom God put forward as an expiation by his
blood, to be received by faith. This was to show God's
righteousness because in his divine forbearance he had passed
over former sins."

What does *hilastērion* mean? Nowadays the A.V.'s "pro-
pitiation" is generally rejected as misleading. The choice
lies between "expiation" and "mercy seat". With the latter

translation, the Cross becomes the place where God's mercy
is offered to sinners. What was once symbolized in the Day
of Atonement ritual (Lev. 16) is now realized in Christ crucified. If we prefer the former, the Cross is the place where
God "expiates", or neutralizes, sin. Either way, Christ
crucified is announced as God's chosen way of mediating
forgiveness to sinners—on the condition of faith—while
at the same time judging sin ("to show God's righteousness"). But we get no clear rationale of the atonement.

II Cor. 5.21 goes deeper. First we are told (v. 14) that
Christ's was an inclusive death ("one has died for all; therefore all have died"), and, then, after stating that the atonement means the cancelling of men's sins, Paul declares that
the crucified Christ, on our behalf, took the whole reality
of sin upon himself, like the scapegoat: "For our sake,
he made him to be sin who knew no sin, so that in him we
might become the righteousness of God." Paul sees the
Cross as an act of God's doing in which the Sinless One,
for the sake of sinners, somehow experienced the horror of
the divine reaction against sin that for us there might be
condemnation no more.

Gal. 3.13 moves in the same realm of ideas. "Christ redeemed us from the curse of the law, having become a curse
for us." The curse is the divine condemnation of sin which
leads to death. To this curse we lay exposed; but Christ on
his Cross so identified himself with the doom impending on
sinners that, through his act, the curse passes away and we
go free.

Such passages show the holy love of God taking awful
issue in the Cross with the sin of man. Christ, by God's
appointing, dies the sinner's death, and so removes sin. Is
there a simpler way of saying this than that Christ bore our
sins? We are not fond nowadays of calling Christ's suffering

"penal" or of styling him our "substitute"; but can we avoid using some such words as these to express Paul's view of the Atonement?

For Paul the Cross is never to be isolated from the Resurrection. "If Christ be not raised, ye are yet in your sins" (I Cor. 15.17). Christ "was delivered up for our trespasses and raised for our justification" (Rom. 4.25). We see the Cross aright only in the light of the Resurrection. We are saved by the living Crucified.

Redemption, justification, reconciliation—such are the three ways in which Paul views salvation as a past event. But man has to make God's gift his own. "Faith" (*pistis*) is the word Paul uses to describe how man appropriates it. Faith is man's response to God's gracious dealing in Christ, and the condition for receiving it.

The word occurs, as noun or verb, nearly two hundred times in his letters. According to the context, it can carry various shades of meaning. It can bear the common Old Testament meaning of "faithfulness" (as in Rom. 3.3.); or confidence in the promises of God (as in Rom. 4.20); or conviction of the unseen—a meaning characteristic of Hebrews—as in II Cor. 5.7; "We walk by faith, not sight." Sometimes it is a synonym for Christianity—as in Rom. 1.8, Gal. 1.23 and 6.10. But the truly Pauline meaning is utter trust—trust with a strong element of obedience (*cf.* Rom. 1.5, which may be translated "the obedience which faith is"). The man who supremely exemplifies Pauline faith in the Old Testament is Abraham who, when God spoke to him, took God at his word and obeyed. Faith, then, for Paul is taking God at his word in Christ. "When a man hears the Gospel and is conquered by it," says Nygren, "that is faith."[1] It is the Yes—the complete response—of the soul to the

[1] *Romans*, 78.

32

grace of God embodied in Christ crucified and risen. This is the faith of which Paul writes in such passages as these:

"By grace are ye saved through faith" (Eph. 2.8).

"Whom God put forward as an expiation by his blood, to be received by faith" (Rom. 3.25).

"For in Christ Jesus you are all sons of God, through faith" (Gal. 3.26).

"He who through faith is righteous shall live" (Rom. 1.17).

This faith we may further characterize thus:

First, it is directed not to a proposition but to a person—sometimes God, as in I Thess. 1.8, sometimes Christ, as in Col. 2.5. But there is no difference of meaning, for Paul's trust is in the God whose glory he has seen in the face of Jesus Christ (II Cor. 4.6).

Second, as the principle of salvation, it is opposed to "works", i.e. every doctrine of redemption by human effort, every attempt by meritorious actions to earn God's favour and lay up credit in the ledgers of heaven (Gal. 2.16; 3.2, Rom. 4.5, etc.).

Third, it is at once an act (Rom. 10.9) and an attitude of life (Gal. 2.20). It is not merely to say once, "I believe in Christ"; it is to go on believing and *living* that. "The life I now live in the flesh," said Paul, "I live by faith in the Son of God who loved me and gave himself for me."

Fourth, faith is, in Luther's figure, the Christian's "wedding-ring". For it so unites a man to Christ that he enters mystically and morally into all that Christ has done for him (Rom. 6.3ff.), so that he dwells in Christ and Christ in him (Gal. 2.20, II Cor. 13.5, Eph. 3.17).

And finally, faith issues in good works. It "works through love" (Gal. 5.6), being itself a response to the love which

3

passes knowledge. Love—obedient, active, self-sacrificing love—is the rose-bloom on Christian faith; and a faith which does not blossom thus is nothing worth (I Cor. 13.2).

Of the reality of this faith baptism is the *seal*. (See Rom. 4.11 and the passages where Paul speaks of Christians being "sealed": II Cor. 1.22, Eph. 1.13; 4.30. In baptism the candidate is stamped as the property of the Lord.)

For Paul, as for his Christian predecessors, baptism was the rite of initiation into the Church. Its mode was immersion. Administered to adults upon profession of their faith ("Jesus is Lord", *cf*. Rom. 10.9: "If you confess with your lips Jesus is Lord . . . you will be saved"), it was "in the name of Christ" (I Cor. 6.11) and was normally associated with the reception of the Holy Spirit (I Cor. 12.13).

In two passages (Rom. 6.3ff. and Col. 2.12) Paul describes baptism as the believer's dying with Christ to sin and rising with him into "newness of life". To understand the "realism" of his language here, we must remember that "behind Christian Baptism stands the 'baptism' of Christ himself (*cf*. Mark 10.38 and Luke 12.50), unique and all-inclusive, undertaken by Christ himself for the sins of the whole world".[1] It is into the virtue of that once-for-all "baptism" that a man enters when he professes his faith in his Lord and is baptized "into Christ".

We must also remember that the physical movements of the rite—descent into the water, immersion and emersion—made a vivid symbol of the thing signified. Only a symbol? No, something more. If Paul's stress on the necessity and primacy of faith precludes the idea that baptism operated by

---

[1] Flemington, *The New Testament Doctrine of Baptism*, 72, *cf*. Cullmann (*Baptism in the New Testament*, 23): "According to the New Testament, all men have in principle received baptism long ago, namely, on Golgotha, at Good Friday and Easter."

a kind of automatic magic, the nature of Old Testament
symbolic actions (what Wheeler Robinson and others have
taught us to call "prophetic symbolism") suggests that for
Paul the very act of baptism set forward—helped to realize—
what it signified, death to the old life and resurrection to the
new. And the baptized person was henceforward under
obligation to become, with the Holy Spirit's help, what in
principle he already was—a new man in Christ.

Chapter Three

SALVATION AS A PRESENT
EXPERIENCE

If a man had been saved when by faith he responded to
God's grace in Christ, it was equally true that he was now
being saved. Salvation was a present and progressive experience.

Our forefathers would have called this the transition from
justification to sanctification. Justification is, in Bunyan's
figure, the wicket-gate admitting to the path towards the
Heavenly City. Sanctification is the path itself. It is the new
Spirit-led life of moral progress, peace and joy—at once,
as the Germans say, *Gabe und Aufgabe*—gift and task.
"Work out your own salvation", Paul says, and in the next
breath, "for God is at work in you" (Phil. 2.13).

Salvation in this aspect Paul describes variously. Believers, he says, are in a new realm—"the kingdom of his
beloved Son" (Col. 1.13). They stand on a new platform,
that of grace—"this grace wherein we stand" (Rom. 5.2).
They are in a new relationship with God, that of adopted
sons, admitted to God's family (Gal. 4.5, Rom. 8.15). Paul
uses the metaphor of adoption to mark the fact that we are
sons of God by grace, whereas Christ is a Son by nature.
(We may recall that in the child-father relation Jesus too saw
the best picture of that fellowship with God, which is man's
true destiny. Note also that both teach that we *become* sons
of God.)

Paul's most positive word for present salvation is Life, the life that is life indeed because lived in the favour and fellowship of God. (Compare St. John's doctrine of "eternal life".) "He who through faith is righteous shall live" (Rom. 1.17). Converted sinners walk "in newness of life" (Rom. 6.4). "Christ died for us", he says, "that, whether we wake or sleep, we should live together with him" (I Thess. 5.10). Ideally—though Paul knows well how far short we come of our high calling—its marks are "death to sin" and "peace with God"—sinlessness and serenity—and it can be described as Life "in Christ" or Life "in the Spirit."

I

Every reader of Paul's letters has noted the frequency of the phrase "in Christ" or "in the Lord" (counting by-forms like "in him", it occurs some 200 times!). What does it mean?

Sometimes the phrase may be no more than a substitute for the word "Christian". Thus Paul calls Onesimus "a beloved brother . . . both in the flesh and in the Lord", which probably means no more than "both as a man and as a Christian". But the phrase carries deeper and richer meanings than this.

Probably it grew out of "baptism into Christ" (Gal. 3.27). When a man was baptized "into Christ", he passed into his possession, became "in him". Whatever else it means, "in Christ" must mean "in communion with Christ". This experience was basic to Paul's Christianity, as it still is to any Christianity worthy of the name. The phrase describes "the most intimate fellowship imaginable of the Christian with the living spiritual Christ"[1] (Deissmann). The Christian,

[1] *St. Paul*, 128.

we may say, lives in a Christ atmosphere. Just as the air we breathe is in us and fills us, and yet we also live and breathe in the air, so is the believer in relation to Christ.

Yet this, while true, is but half the truth. In many passages "in Christ" clearly has a communal significance. The clue is to be sought in the Hebrew idea of "corporate personality" —a conception which enabled him to think of the community in terms of its representative head; and we may remember that in the Old Testament the Messiah could be equated with Israel (see Ps. 28.8 and 89.38). Now we know Paul thought of Christ in this corporate way, witness I Cor. 12.12: "For just as the body is one and has many members, and all the members of the body, though many, are one body, so it is with Christ." "Paul calls Christ the Church", says Calvin, and he is right.

We have to say then that the phrase means not only "in communion with Christ" but also "in the community of Christ". It implies membership in the Church, which is Christ's Body. So Floyd Filson[1] writes: "To be 'in Christ', while it is a great personal experience and privilege, is a privilege which inevitably puts a man into Church and binds him to his fellow-believers in the one body of Christ." G. S. Duncan[2] makes the same point: "Christ and his People form a corporate fellowship, so that to be 'in Christ' means to be a member of that religious fellowship which draws its very life from Christ." In fine, Pauline "mysticism" is no "flight of the alone to the Alone". It is a social experience. It is to have discovered true community—in Christ. This is the key to such passages as:

"Ye are all one (man) in Christ" (Gal. 3.28).

"In Christ Jesus neither circumcision nor uncircumcision is of any avail" (Gal. 5.6).

[1] *The New Testament against its Environment*, 77.   [2] *Galatians*, 104.

"There is therefore now no condemnation to those who are in Christ Jesus" (Rom. 8.1).

"As in Adam all die, so also in Christ shall all be made alive" (I Cor. 15.22).

Note

Deissmann probably erred in taking the phrase to be Paul's own coinage. (1) The idea is implicit in the Synoptic doctrine of the solidarity of the Messiah with his People; *cf.* Mark 8.38: "Whoever is ashamed of me and mine, etc." (the reading of W and k). (2) Sayings like Matt 18.20 and 25.40–45 contain it in germ. (3) The phrase, or its equivalent, occurs in John, Acts and I Peter.

2

But to be "in Christ" was equally to be "in the Spirit". (Note how often the phrase "in the Spirit" is found with the same verbs and nouns as the phrase "in Christ". "Sanctified in the Holy Spirit" (Rom. 15.16) is paralleled by "sanctified in Christ Jesus" (I Cor. 1.2), as "joy in the Holy Spirit" (Rom. 14.17) by "rejoice in the Lord" (Phil. 3.1), and so on.) Yet, in spite of the statement, "The Lord is the Spirit" (II Cor. 3.17), Paul does not identify Christ with the Spirit. The truth is rather that it is through the Spirit that Christ comes to the Christian. Experientially, they are one.

For Paul, the Holy Spirit is *the divine dynamic* of the new life (see I Thess. 1.5 and Rom. 15.13): it is God's gracious power operating on and in man, yet never apart from Christ. This is why he can speak indifferently of "the Spirit of God" "the Spirit of Christ" and "Christ in you" (Rom. 8.9f.), meaning the self-same power. And always the Spirit stands for what we call the supernatural: not only God as a presence in man but God as a power transcending human experience.

Paul, of course, did not originate belief in the Holy Spirit. The Pentecostal Event (Acts 2) had made the Christian community signally aware of a strange new "uprush of life" in their midst, which they identified with the Spirit of God promised for "the last days" (Joel 2). But whereas the first Christians regarded the Spirit chiefly as the source of ecstatic religious "experiences" like "tongues" and what we would call "revival phenomena", Paul saw it as the source of all religious experience, and of gifts which, if less spectacular, were more serviceable.[1] So he notably advanced Christian thinking about it. By "playing down" the less wholesome evidences of the Spirit, he helped to *moralize* men's thinking about it. By his conception of the Spirit as "leading", "witnessing" and "pleading" he helped to *personalize* their thought about it. And by linking the Spirit with the living Christ, he helped to *christianize* their thoughts. Paul's "fruits of the Spirit", as Schleiermacher rightly observed, "are the virtues of Christ" (Gal. 5.22).

How wonderfully wide and rich is his whole conception of the Spirit! Sharply opposed to "the flesh" and to "the law" the Spirit creates power where there was weakness, freedom where there was servitude, holiness where there was "flesh of sin" and life where there was death. It is the Spirit which brings home to our hearts the love of God for sinners in Christ crucified (Rom. 5.5); which enables us to fulfil "the just demands of the law" and live righteously (Rom. 8.4); which teaches us to say, "Abba, Father" (Rom. 8.15f.); and which helps us when we stumble in our prayers

[1] It is clear from I Cor. 12–14 that if Paul had been compelled to arrange the gifts of the Spirit in order of merit, "love" would have stood first and *glōssolalia* last.

(Rom. 8.26). As the "first instalment" of our heavenly inheritance (II Cor. 1.22; 5.5), it is the Spirit which creates in us "immortal longings"; for our hope is that he who raised Christ from the dead by his powerful Spirit will also quicken us to everlasting life by that same Spirit (Rom. 8.11).

To sum up. The Spirit is God in Christ at work in men, helping, inspiring, quickening, sanctifying. The Christian life is a life lived by its beneficent energy. And, as the phrase "the fellowship of the Spirit"[1] implies, the Spirit "knows nothing of solitary Christianity" but binds all sorts and conditions of men together in the bonds of Christian "togetherness". The man who would know how central the Spirit is to Paul's Christianity should ponder well Gal. 5, II Cor. 3 and Rom. 8, not forgetting I Cor. 12–14, which treat of the Spirit's gifts. There the whole Christian life is Spirit-controlled. Living, suffering, praying, hoping—all is guided, prompted and secured by the strong Spirit of God.

3

If the Spirit is the dynamic of the new life, the *sphere* in which it is lived is the Church.

The Church began when Jesus called twelve men to be the nucleus of the new Israel, and for Paul the Church is basically a pure communion of persons bound to Christ and to one another through the Holy Spirit. He calls it by various names: "the saints" "the household of faith" "the temple of God" and, in a nuptial symbol, the bride of Christ. But he thinks of it in two principal ways.

To begin with, it is the true People of God. Israel after the flesh, claiming to be God's People, have forfeited their

---

[1] II Cor. 13.14 (*cf.* Phil. 2.1). The phrase means either (*a*) fellowship created by the Spirit, or (*b*) fellowship in (participation in) the Spirit.

claim by rejecting the Messiah, and the Christians have served themselves heirs to it. Once only (Gal. 6.16) he calls it "the Israel of God", but it is of the Church as the true People of God he is thinking when he claims, "We are the circumcision" (Phil. 3.3), or calls Christians "the seed of Abraham" (Gal. 3.29), or likens the Church to an Olive Tree with its native and its wild shoots (Rom. 11.17–24). These phrases underscore the continuity of the Church with the ancient People of God. But the Church is no less a new creation, reconstituted by the blood of the New Covenant at the Last Supper and inaugurated by the Resurrection and the gift of the Spirit. For this new creation, the old ceremonial laws are no longer valid, and with the abolition of "the middle wall of partition" between Jew and Gentile, nationality has ceased to count: open to all who have faith, the potential bounds of the new People of God are as wide as mankind.

The same claim is also contained in Paul's use of the word *Ecclesia*. In the Septuagint the word had denoted the People of God assembled for common action. By applying it to themselves, Christ's followers claimed to be the true People of God. Sometimes Paul calls the Church simply "the *Ecclesia*"; sometimes he speaks in the plural of "*the ecclesiae*." Sometimes he means the whole number of Christians when he says *Ecclesia*; oftener he refers to the local congregation —the word "Corinth" or "Galatia" being added. But the point to remember is that, for Paul, the inclusive "People-of-God" sense is primary. Each local congregation is an outcrop, or embodiment, of the one great company of God's elect People who worship him through Christ in the power of the Holy Spirit.

St. Paul's most characteristic and original name for the Church is "the Body of Christ" (see Rom. 12.4f., I Cor.

12.12ff., Col. 1.18, 24; 2.19 and Ephesians *passim*). This title, defining the Church in terms of Christ, shows that Paul's ecclesiology is a branch of his Christology. (To say, as is often said, that the Church is the Extension of the Incarnation is a dangerous way of putting it. The Word made flesh was sinless. The Church is not.)

We cannot be sure whence Paul took the name. One guess (Rawlinson's) is that he derived it from the imagery of the Eucharist in which Christians are one body by partaking of the one loaf signifying Christ's body: "Because there is one loaf", says Paul, "we, the many, (partaking of it) are one body" (I Cor. 10.17). Another guess (favoured by W. L. Knox and others) is that Paul was adapting an older Stoic employment of the word *sōma* to describe a commonwealth. Whatever his source, Paul quite literally baptized it "into Christ", for in his usage the stress falls on the words "of Christ". Christians are *his* Body, the sphere of action of his risen life.

Doubtless the Hebrew conception of "corporate personality" helped Paul to think along these lines. (Acts 9.4: "Saul, Saul, why persecutest thou *me?*" indicates the solidarity between the risen Christ and his People.) To understand Paul's teaching, we have to remember not only that a man's body is the instrument whereby he communicates with the external world, but also that the early Christians had a vivid sense of the living Christ working in their community through the Spirit. So Paul conceived of the Church as the Body of the Risen Lord—a social organism made up of many members, indwelt by the risen Christ, and carrying out his purposes in the world as once his physical body had done in Galilee and Judea.

As Paul works out his theology of the Body, it has both a vertical and a horizontal reference. On the one hand, the

Body looks up to Christ as its Head and Saviour (Col. 1.18, Eph. 1.22) from whom it draws its vitality (Col. 2.19, Eph. 4.16). On the other, those who are in Christ's Body are members one of the other, with gifts which vary but are all needed for the good of the whole (Rom. 12.4ff., I Cor. 12.12ff.).

The depth and richness of this doctrine is clear. It stresses the headship of Christ, whilst emphasizing the closeness of his union with believers, and their unity in him. It brings out their interdependence. And it finely sets forth the Church's vocation—a vocation magnificently elaborated in Ephesians—as the organism which is to carry out his purposes in the world. The Church is the continuator of the Messianic Ministry of Jesus, called, like him, by service and suffering, to spread the Reign of God to the ends of the earth, till all men are reconciled to him through Christ.[1]

4

The doctrine of the Church as the Body of Christ leads on to the rite in which it was symbolized.

For St. Paul, the Lord's Supper was the "supernatural[2] food and drink" of the new life (I Cor. 10.3). As Baptism was the sacrament of initiation, so the Supper was the sacrament of continuing fellowship. Here in an act, repeated in obedience to the Lord's command, the Church realized itself as a fellowship with and in Christ.

Our sources (I Cor. 10.1–4, 14–22; 11.17–33) are scanty and hard to interpret; but clearly for the Apostle the Supper was more than a memorial meal: it was a sacrament with past, present and future aspects.

[1] See T. W. Manson, *The Church's Ministry*, 24.
[2] *pneumatikos*. Since Paul is speaking of material realities, "spiritual" is a misleading translation.

First, it was a proclamation, a *verbum visibile*, of the death of Christ. "Ye proclaim the Lord's death", Paul told the Corinthians. The rite rested on "the finished work" of Christ on the Cross, and looked back to it.

But it was more than sacred retrospection. It was a communion with the living Christ in his character as crucified. This is the meaning of I Cor. 10.16f. "The cup of blessing which we bless, is it not a participation (*koinōnia*) in the blood of Christ? The bread which we break, is it not a participation in the body of Christ?" The root idea of *koinōnia* is not so much that of association with other persons as that of sharing in something wherein others also share. What is the something here? It is, first, "the blood of Christ"—a vivid metaphor for his redemptive death; and, second, it is "the body of Christ", i.e. the person of Christ. When Christians partake of this food and drink (Paul would say) there is set up the closest fellowship with the Saviour Christ and (as he adds in the next verse) with one another. Christ is the Host at his Table, and the worshippers share in the virtue of all that he has done for them. Here "divine materialism and divine socialism unite", for in eating the bread and drinking the wine Christ is in their midst and in consequence they become one body.

But, third, the Supper was a prophecy—it was a foretaste, pointing forward to the perfected communion in glory—"till he come" (I Cor. 11.26).

5

We come finally to the moral issues of the new life—to the Pauline Ethic.

For St. Paul, "truth is always truth in order to goodness". In other words, Christian ethics grow out of Christian doctrine. One is the root, the other is the fruit. Thus, to take a typical example, Col. 1–2 expounds the theology, Col. 3–4 the ethic, beginning: "If then you have been raised with Christ, seek the things that are above." First, doctrine, then the moral issues flowing from it—such is Paul's way. What he says, in effect, is this: "You are now new men in Christ: see to it that you behave like them."

The next point is that Paul is not a systematic moralist on the classical pattern. He does not, like the Greek moralists, talk about the *summum bonum* or compile lists of the cardinal virtues—justice, prudence, temperance and fortitude, and so on. For him, Christian life is life in the Spirit, whose final aim is Christlikeness. Christian behaviour is the spontaneous expression of the new Spirit-controlled life given by God in Christ. It is a life of freedom from the law as an external code or control; for external controls are off and internal controls—those of the Spirit—are on. Yet it is not antinomian, for the Spirit lays down the proper course of conduct for man to follow, and justice is done to the demands of the law only by those who walk after the Spirit (Rom. 8.4). Moreover, if the Christian is free, there are limits to his freedom. If "all things are permitted", yet everyone is to seek not his own good but that of others (Phil. 2.4), and love must have priority over liberty: "Therefore if food is a cause of my brother's falling, I will never eat meat, lest I cause my brother to fall" (I Cor. 8.13).

Nor is this Spirit-led life without its standards. Paramount is the example of Christ; and in three famous passages Paul holds it up for the Christian's imitation. In Rom. 15.3 we are told "Christ did not please himself". No more should we. In II Cor. 8.9, urging the Corinthians to be generous, Paul says: "You know the grace of our Lord Jesus Christ, that though he was rich, yet for your sake he became poor."

And in Phil. 2.5 the self-denial of Christ becomes a pattern for Paul's readers: "Have this mind among yourselves which you have in Christ Jesus"—the Christ who renounced "the form of God" that he might take the form of a servant.

The dominant principle of Paul's ethic is *Agapē*: a word hard to render because "charity" is nowadays so restricted in its meaning and "love" can cover all kinds of affection "from Hollywood to heaven". If we retain "love" as a translation, the English word "caring" often comes nearest the meaning.

Like his Lord, Paul made *Agapē* the master-key of morals. (Noun and verb occur some ninety-five times in his letters, excluding the Pastoral Epistles.) As the sole universally valid precept Jesus ever gave was, "Thou shalt love", so Paul with the mind of his Master says, "The greatest of these (spiritual gifts) is love" (I Cor. 13.13). "Above all, put on love which is the perfect link" (Col. 3.14). Love, in fact, is "the sum-total of the law" (Rom. 13.10, *cf.* Gal. 5.14) because anyone who acts under its impulse will not wish to injure his neighbour by stealing, killing, coveting or adultery.

What is *Agapē*? It is not *erōs* (a word not found in the New Testament), the love which desires and at its lowest lusts. It is not *philia*, "friendship", the affection which binds together kindred souls like David and Jonathan. *Agapē* is the love which seeks not to possess but to give. "*Erōs* is all take; *philia* is give and take; *agapē* is all give."[1] It is no mere emotion or sentiment; rather is it a new way of living for our fellow-men because God has so loved us in Christ. "We love because he first loved us." It is the response of hearts which have been exposed in Christ to the love which

[1] G. B. Caird.

passes knowledge. It is the energy which Christians are required to radiate among their fellow-men. They are to "truth it in love" (Eph. 4.15), remembering that if "knowledge puffs up, love builds up" (I Cor. 8.1). For the rest, the necessity, the nature and the never-failingness of love are imperishably depicted in St. Paul's "song of songs", I Cor. 13.

Love then for Paul (as for Henry Drummond) was "the greatest thing in the world". His general view of what moralists call "the Good" can be seen in his description of "the fruits of the Spirit" (Gal. 5.22). First comes "love"; then "joy" which is not merely *joie de vivre* but the deep feeling that life means good, born of faith in God; then "peace", that serenity of mind springing from a right relationship with God; then "long temper" (*makrothumia*), which is the happy opposite of "short temper"; then "kindness"; then "goodness" which is "righteousness plus" (Rom. 5.7), righteousness informed by love; then "faith", i.e. fidelity or reliability; then "gentleness", or considerateness for others; and finally "self-control" (*enkrateia*) which is a word of far wider scope than our "temperance".

A final word on Paul's social ethics. The emergence of specific moral problems in his churches, notably at Corinth, compelled the Apostle to give specific duties and directions. Sometimes in these judgments he appears very much as a man of his time; far oftener he commands our admiration by his sanctified common sense. Let us note what he has to say about the family, woman, marriage, slavery and the State.

In several letters he lays down "household rules" to regulate relations between husbands and wives, parents and children, masters and slaves. Much of this probably came from the common apostolic catechesis—a body of ethical

material drawn from Hellenistic Judaism but suitably chris-
tianized and reinforced, as we can see in Rom. 12–14, by
the moral teaching of Jesus.

In his view of woman Paul sometimes hardly rises above
the contemporary evaluation of her as "an inferior being"
(see I Cor. 11.3, 9, Eph. 5.23). But Gal. 3.28 shows that he
knew where the logic of the Faith ought to lead him: "There
is neither male nor female, for you are all one in Christ
Jesus." Critics have said that in I Cor. 7 he regards marriage
as very much "a second best". This is fair enough, but we
shall do well to hold Paul to his more human and truly
Christian teaching in Eph. 5.21–23, where "the pure love
of a man and a woman is a sacrament of the divine love of
Christ, and the marriage relation which it consecrates
is indissoluble".[1]

It has been complained that he leaves the institution of
slavery uncriticized; yet he demands a square deal for the
slave from his master ("Masters, treat your slaves justly and
fairly, knowing that you also have a master in heaven" (Col.
4.1)); and his handling of the problem of the runaway
Onesimus points the way to the true Christian solution:
"Take him back", he advises Philemon, "no longer as a
slave, but as a brother beloved."

Lastly, in one passage he enunciates the Christian attitude
to the State (Rom. 13.1–7). Christians are to be subject to
the civil authorities and to pay their taxes. As the powerful
ally of the law-abiding man, and the foe of the anti-social
person the State performs the will of God and can be
described as divinely ordained.

---

[1] C. H. Dodd, *The Meaning of Paul for Today*, 150.

Chapter Four

SALVATION AS A
FUTURE HOPE

"We were saved", "We are being saved", "We shall be saved"—these are the three tenses of salvation. To be a Christian, as Brunner has said,[1] is to share in "something which has happened, which is happening and which will happen". Our concern now is with the third of the three tenses—with what is going to happen, with the consummation of the new life which the man in Christ now enjoys.

What did Paul teach about the Last Things? Eschatology there is in plenty in St. Paul's letters, but no single, clear, unvarying scheme with the time-table of future events finally fixed and the topography of the unseen world precisely charted. Indeed, in these high and mysterious matters the Apostle's insight seems to have deepened and developed with the passage of the years. What strikes us in the earliest letters, I and II Thessalonians (written roughly about A.D. 50) is his debt to Jewish apocalyptic and his hope of a speedy and dramatic Second Advent of Christ. In his Prison Epistles, written about a dozen years later, while the hope of Christ's Coming remains, Paul dwells more and more on the divine blessings which the Christian already enjoys. Still, the Apostle has certain large and clear convictions about the Christian Hope in all his writings, and it is with these rather than with details we are now concerned.

[1] *Man in Revolt*, 494.

1. Our first point must be that for Paul, as for all the early Christians, the Last Things are in a true sense already here. The "fullness of time" has come, and the *Eschaton* has entered history. Christ has died and risen, inaugurating the new order of things, and now at the right hand of God reigns over the Church and the world, albeit his is a hidden kingship. The future has in a real sense become present. In principle, the Christian has begun to enter on his glorious inheritance. Even now he possesses the love of God, and nothing that is to come, nothing in this world or out of it, can rob him of it. Already Christians are "risen with Christ", having been "translated out of the kingdom of darkness into the kingdom of God's beloved Son." Already they have been "acquitted", and need not wait for God's finalizing verdict on Judgment Day. Already they possess the Spirit, promised for the last days, and it is the pledge of full salvation. To be sure, since they are still "in the flesh", redemption is not complete, and they are still summoned to work out their own salvation in fear and trembling, striving against all the powers of evil still existent in the world; but their sense of "peace with God", their faith-life with the risen and regnant Christ, and the fruits of the Spirit are sure tokens that they are already enjoying the blessings of the Kingdom which has come with the coming of Christ:

> *The men of grace have found*
> *Glory begun below.*

(This is Paul's characteristic teaching, if it is not conspicuous in his earliest letters. You may note the change of stress if you compare the Thessalonian letters with, say, Colossians which is almost certainly one of his last. In the letters to Thessalonica the emphasis falls on the future, and Paul's picture of the Last Things—the sounding trumpet, the archangel's voice, the flaming fire, etc.—is painted in the conventional colours of Jewish apocalyptic. It is much different in Colossians. Christians are already in Christ's kingdom and risen with him, though their hope of final blessedness, now "laid up in heaven", as Paul puts it, must wait till "Christ, who is our life, appears.")

2. But Paul's eschatology was not all realised—far from it. What had happened through God's act in Christ, what he was now experiencing, was but prelude and pledge of something far more glorious. If D-Day had dawned (to borrow Cullmann's analogy), the coming of V-Day, the day of final Victory, was assured. Amid all awareness of present blessing there shone for him, like a brilliant star, the hope of the day of final redemption—the Day of Christ or the Parousia—when Christ would be unveiled in his glory, the dead would rise, the Judgment would take place, and the faithful would gain "glory and honour and immortality".

It is clear, from his earlier letters at any rate, that Paul expected that day soon—in his own lifetime—but, come it soon or late, it would mean the destruction of sin and death and the consummation of God's saving purpose for men in Christ.

This hope of Christ's "royal coming", then, pervades all his letters—the chief passages being I Thess. 4, II Thess. 1–2, I Cor. 15 and II Cor. 5—and if it is not easy to reconcile in one harmonious whole all that he has to say about it at various times (Paul was primarily a missionary, not a systematic theologian) certain things are clear enough. For one thing, Paul thinks primarily not of individual immortality but of a cosmic salvation, and in one passage—Rom. 8.8–25 —his hope embraces not only the redemption of "the sons of God" but the renovation of the whole creation. For a second thing, the Consummation must include Judgment.

"God", says Paul, "shall judge the secrets of men by Christ Jesus" (Rom. 2.16). (In Rom. 14.10 Paul speaks of "the judgment seat of God", in II Cor. 5.10 of "the judgment seat of Christ".) All must give an account. Only, "there is now no condemnation for those that are in Christ Jesus" (Rom. 8.1). "Who shall lay anything to the charge of God's elect?" (Rom. 8.33). The Christian, already acquitted by God's grace, may face the tribunal in that assurance. Finally, the Coming will mean the open triumph of Christ and his saints —the revealing of the hidden-ness of the Easter triumph— and the defeat of all evil, that God may be "all in all".

3. This leads to the third main point in Paul's eschatology. The heart of his Christian hope can be put in three words: "being with Christ".

Christ, "the first born among many brethren", is already risen and regnant. He is "the first fruits". What happened to him will happen also to those who are "in Christ"; for we are joint-heirs with Christ, and if we have died with Christ, we believe that we shall also live with him (Rom. 6.8). "So shall we always be with the Lord" (I Thess. 4.17). "My desire is to depart and be with Christ" (Phil. 1.23). "The future", it has been said, "which means being 'with Christ' is the culmination of the present which means being 'in Christ'." And this hope, it must be added, is not only of being with Christ but of being like him; for the Christian's destiny is to be "conformed to the image of his Son" (Rom. 8.29. *cf.* I John 3.2).

4. If the heart of the Christian hope is being with Christ, its secret—its condition—is being "in Christ". "For as in Adam all die, even so in Christ shall all be made alive" (I Cor. 15.22). "Those who are fallen asleep in Christ shall God bring with him" (I Thess. 4.14. *cf.* Rom. 8.11). But what of mankind at large? What of the rebellious and

apostate? In the Thessalonian letters Paul could foresee nothing but "eternal destruction" for those who rejected Christ (I Thess. 1.9). Yet when he comes to write Romans about seven years later, reluctant to believe that his "kinsmen according to the flesh" will be finally lost, he moves to some sort of a "larger hope" (Rom. 11.32)—a view which seems to widen still further in Colossians and Ephesians where God's purpose, according to the Apostle, is "to reconcile to himself all things, whether in earth or in heaven" (Col. 1.20, *cf.* Eph. 1.10). Yet it would be hazardous to interpret Paul's "God will have mercy on all" as proof that he is a "universalist" in the modern dogmatic sense. Elsewhere (II Cor. 2.13f.) he distinguishes between those who are being "saved" and those who are "perishing" and in the Romans passage he is thinking in terms of races rather than of individuals. To find here the dogmatic assertion that every man, no matter what his sins, will at last receive mercy and reach heaven, is to say something which is probably not true of Paul and certainly not of the rest of the New Testament.

5. The mode of the Christian's heavenly life is "a spiritual body" (I Cor. 15, II Cor. 5.1ff., Phil. 3.20f.).

Paul holds that the life to come is a gift of God, not (as the Greeks held) a natural possession of man. Not the immortality of the soul but the resurrection of the body is his concern and hope. But when he uses the word "body" (*sōma*), he is not thinking of it as we do, or hoping for any revivification of our physical make-up. "Flesh and blood", he says explicitly, "cannot inherit the kingdom of God" (I Cor. 15.50). For Paul, the "body" is the organic principle of identity which persists through the years and all changes of substance. "Organism" or "frame" perhaps best gives the meaning. Now the body has a material means of expression;

hereafter God will give it a new embodiment befitting the heavenly world—a body of glory, a spirit-body. Our lowly bodies will be changed to resemble Christ's glorious body (Phil. 3.21)—the body invested with the glory of another world which he had seen on the Damascus Road. For "as we have borne the image of the man of dust [Adam], so also we shall bear the image of the man of heaven [Christ]" (I Cor. 15.49). Of Paul's conception we may say two things. First, it assures us that the personality is renewed after death not as a ghost but with all that is needed for its self-expression and its power to communicate with others. Second, it avoids the drawbacks of both the Greek and the Jewish views. The Greek doctrine of the immortality of the soul secured spirituality but endangered personal identity. The Jewish doctrine preserved identity but imperilled spirituality.[1]

When does the great change take place? In I Thess. 4.15–17 and I Cor. 15.51f. Paul expects it on "the day of Christ". But in II Cor. 5.1ff., he apparently holds that it is at death that the new body is assumed, and in Phil. 1.23 he speaks of "departing and being with the Lord". But, come the change when it may, the redemption of the body is certain.

In his teaching about the Last Things Paul is aware that "we know only in part" and that our knowledge here is like vision through an unclear mirror (I Cor. 13.12). That complete redemption awaits all who are Christ's, he is sure, as that in the end God will be "all in all". Beyond this Paul does not go. A strong faith is not curious about details. It is enough to know that "this corruptible must put on incorruption, and this mortal immortality" (I Cor. 15.53).

And with God be the rest.

[1] J. S. Stewart, *A Man in Christ*, 268.

Chapter Five

THE SAVIOUR

We have outlined Paul's doctrine of salvation. Its source was God, its mediator Christ. "For us", he says, "there is one God, the Father, from whom are all things and for whom we exist, and one Lord, Jesus Christ, through whom are all things and through whom we exist" (I Cor. 8.6). Remembering that "Paul is not so much the great *Christologos* as the great *Christophoros*"[1]—that his prime concern is to preach Christ as an evangelist rather than to expound his nature as a systematic theologian—we have to ask finally, How does St. Paul think of Christ?

Before we attempt an answer, there are two prior questions to be faced. The first is: How much did Paul know of the historic Jesus, the Jesus whose work and words are known to us from the Gospels? The opinion is widely current that because Paul's eyes of faith are fixed on the living and exalted Lord, and because he says relatively little in his letters about the Ministry of Jesus, he knew next to nothing about that Jesus. We think this highly improbable. When this question is discussed, it is important to remember the very obvious point, that Paul's writings are Epistles, not Gospels, and that his readers are converts who already knew the main facts about Christ, having heard them in the *kērygma*. We must also remember that Paul numbered among his friends and coadjutors (John Mark, Simon Peter

[1] Deissmann, *The Religion of Jesus and the Faith of Paul*, 189.

and James, the Lord's brother, to name only three) men who had been eyewitnesses of Jesus in the days of his flesh and who could correct or supplement that knowledge of Jesus which he must have had even before his conversion. And, finally, it is very easy to forget, or underrate the amount of information about the historic Jesus to be gleaned from a patient sifting of the Epistles themselves.

Let this summary suffice now. Jesus was a man (Gal. 4.4), born of David's line (Rom. 1.3). He had brothers (Gal. 1.19, I Cor. 9.5). His ministry was to the Jews (Rom. 15.8), as his earthly lot was that of a poor man (II Cor. 8.9). Before the Jews killed him (I Thess. 2.15), he instituted "the Lord's Supper" (I Cor. 11.23ff.). He was crucified and "buried" (the verb indicates that he knew the story of Joseph of Arimathea), and on the third day rose from the dead and appeared to many witnesses (I Cor. 15.3ff., II Cor. 13.4). Nor is Paul ignorant of Jesus' character. He was meek and gentle (II Cor. 10.1, *cf.* Matt. 11.29); obedient to his Father's will (Rom. 5.19, Phil. 2.8); of a steadfast endurance (II Thess. 3.5); and unacquainted with sin (II Cor. 5.21). And when in I Cor. 13.4–7 Paul limns the features of *agapē*, can we doubt who it was sat in the studio of his imagination for that portrait?[1]

As for Christ's teaching, Paul can quote, when need demands it, sayings of the Lord (I Cor. 7.10; 9.14 and Acts 20.35). Elsewhere Paul's own teaching unmistakably echoes his Lord at point after point: on returning good for evil (Rom. 12.14, 17 and I Cor. 4.12); on the paying of taxes (Rom. 13.7); on the sin of censorious judging (Rom. 14.4, 10, 13); on mountain-moving faith (I Cor. 13.2), not to mention passages like Rom. 8.5, Col. 3.13 and II Thess. 3.3 which seem to show his knowledge of the Lord's prayer.

[1] John Baillie, *The Place of Jesus Christ in Modern Christianity*, 81.

But enough has been quoted to indicate how baseless is the charge that Paul knew little or nothing of the historic Jesus.

We may turn now to the second question: How is Paul's Christ related to the Christ of the Synoptic Gospels?

Fifty years ago, when theological Liberalism was in the ascendancy, the charge was often made that Paul had turned the peasant-preacher of God's Fatherhood into a cosmic redeemer—that between the historic Jesus and the Pauline Christ a great gulf was fixed.

Nowadays no self-respecting scholar lightly levels that charge. The idea is now discredited that "beneath the surface of the Gospels we can unearth a purely human prophet of the Divine Fatherhood and human brotherhood who was transformed by St. Paul into a supernatural Saviour".[1] Various factors have led to this result.

To begin with, the rediscovery and better understanding of the eschatological element in the Gospels has had its effect. Not only has it shown the Liberal picture of Jesus to be false, but it has revealed the Jesus of the Gospels to be an immeasurably greater person than the Liberals had supposed —to be indeed the all-decisive person at a supreme crisis in God's dealings with men.

In the second place, scholars (like Denney in his *Jesus and the Gospel*) who studied afresh the self-revelation of Jesus in the Gospels recalled us to one who knew himself to be the Son of God in a unique and lonely sense. We began to see that the Christology of Jesus himself was not unworthy to bear the weight of the claims made for him by St. Paul.

And, thirdly, the gulf which had seemed to yawn between Paul and the earliest Christians was wellnigh bridged. We had learned how much Paul owed to his seniors in Christ. If Paul set Jesus on the divine side of reality, so did they.

[1] Alec Vidler, *Christian Belief*, 48.

If he declared that his was the only name under heaven
whereby men might be saved, no less did they. Paul and the
Jerusalem leaders may have clashed on other issues. There
is not a scrap of evidence that they ever clashed on the
supreme issue of Christology. The Christ Paul preached
was the same Christ as his precursors preached. Paul's was a
greater Christ only in the sense that Paul interpreted him by
new needs, relating him to the religious yearnings not of
Judaism only but of the great Gentile world which he was
called to evangelize. In short, historic Christianity stems
from Jesus, not Paul; but Paul was the first to grasp fully
the true magnitude of his person; and for this all succeeding
Christian generations have been his debtors.

We are ready now to study Paul's view of Christ.

"Life means Christ to me", he said once (Phil. 1.21).
Does this mean that for him Christ has usurped the place of
God? No; rather it is God who meets men in Christ, the
same God who once acted in creation. "It is the God who
said, 'Let light shine out of darkness' who has shone in our
hearts to give the light of the knowledge of the glory of
God in the face of Christ" (II Cor. 4.6). But this God is
only surely accessible to sinful man in Christ. One may
know something of God from his creation—glimpse his
power and deity (Rom. 1.20); and one may discern his
sovereign will for men in the law; but neither in nature nor in
law but only in Christ is God savingly known. For in Christ,
God, of his grace, draws near to sinful men and stretches
out his saving hand. And this Christ, as Paul's letters testify
on every page, is no mere figure in past history, but a living
and delivering Presence who dwells in the believer's heart
through faith and the power of the Spirit. This is God's
great secret, as Paul tells the Colossians (1.27) long hid but
now disclosed: "Christ in you, the hope of glory."

Of this Christ, crucified, risen and regnant, Paul is the herald and ambassador; yet his "Christophory" implies a "Christology", and we must now sum it up.

Paul affirms the full humanity of Christ: "born of a woman, born under the law" (Gal. 4.4): "For as by a man came death, by a man came also the resurrection of the dead" (I Cor. 15.21): Christ came "in the likeness of sinful flesh" (Rom. 8.3), that is, in a life incarnate but sinless. No less certainly, however, Paul sets him on the divine side of reality, conjoining his name with the name of God at point after point. Once he seems to call him "God" (Rom. 9.5); yet if this interpretation is rejected, as it often is, Paul makes claims for Christ hardly less exalted. He is the God-man: "in him dwells the plenitude of deity, corporeally," i.e. within the physical limits God set himself in the Incarnation (Col. 2.9). If he subordinates Christ to God the Father— "the head of Christ is God" (I Cor. 11.3, *cf.* I Cor. 3.23 and 15.28)—he does not scruple to apply to Christ titles and words used in the Old Testament of the All Highest (Rom. 10.13, I Cor. 1.2). He conceives of Christ as having pre-existed (I Cor. 10.4, Gal. 4.4, Phil. 2.6). He links Christ with the Holy Spirit, and though probably not identifying them, he can say of Christ, "The last Adam became a life-giving Spirit" (I Cor. 15.45, *cf.* II Cor. 3.17). But perhaps the most staggering claim he makes is when he assigns Christ a *cosmic* role, finding in him the key to creation, declaring that it is all there with Christ in view. "For us", he says, "there is one Lord Jesus Christ, through whom are all things and through whom we exist" (I Cor. 8.6). And if we are tempted to judge this a mere *obiter dictum* to the Corinthians, not to be taken too seriously, we are prevented by Col. 1.15–18, where Paul, in face of the Colossian "theosophists" who were busy scaling down his significance, reinterprets the whole universe in the light of Christ:

"He is the image of the invisible God, the first-born of all creation; for in him all things were created, in heaven and on earth, visible and invisible, whether thrones or dominions or principalities or authorities—all things were created through him and for him. He is before all things, and in him all things hold together."

The man who wrote these words believed that embedded in the constitution of creation itself was a reference to the Person and Sovereignty of Christ.

After all this any enumeration of the titles Paul applies to Jesus may seem almost unnecessary.

From the day of his conversion Paul had no doubt Jesus was the Messiah (Acts 9.22). "All the promises of God", he said, "find their Yes in him" (II Cor. 1.20). Yet though in one or two places he employs the word "Christ" in its official sense[1]—the clearest is Rom. 9.5—he does not labour the proof of Jesus' Messiahship, clearly because the word "Messiah" would have conveyed as much to his Gentile hearers as the word "Mahdi" conveys to English audiences today; probably too because he knew no racial or traditional categories could confine the Redeemer—he belonged not to Israel but to mankind.

Paul's favourite title for Christ was "the Lord" (*ho Kyrios*) or "our Lord", a title which meant much for Gentile ears and gave Christ an exalted religious significance.

Paul was not the first to apply it to Christ. The Aramaic-speaking Church's watchword "*Marana tha*" ("Our Lord,

[1] "In the Epistles Paul never says 'Jesus is the Christ' . . . He never seems to have laid much stress on teaching the Gentiles the meaning of the name. But his whole work as an apostle is conditioned by the Messiahship of Jesus." N. A. Dahl in *Studia Paulina*, 94.

come!" (I Cor. 16.22)) shows that Paul's predecessors had given Jesus "the name which is above every name"; and it is likely that "Jesus is Lord" was the earliest Christian confession of faith (*cf.* Rom. 10.9 and I Cor. 12.3). This title which in the Septuagint stood for the ineffable name of God, set Jesus incontrovertibly on the side of deity, and into it Paul poured all the wealth of his devotion. It set forth his own relation to Jesus: Jesus was the Lord; he was the bond-slave of this Lord. And the aim of all his apostolic labours was to bring men into this relationship. "For we preach not ourselves but Christ Jesus as Lord, and ourselves as your servants for Jesus' sake" (II Cor. 4.5).

Paul had a third great title for Christ. "I live", he wrote, "by faith in the Son of God who loved me and gave himself for me" (Gal. 2.20). Jesus was "Son"—the Son of God in a special sense.

We know from the Gospels that Jesus had so designated himself (Luke 10.22, Q; Mark 12.6; 13.32). Since Paul never argues for his ascription of divine sonship to Jesus, we may infer that he took the title, via the Church's tradition, from Jesus' own usage. In all, he employs it seventeen times. Sometimes it may mean no more than Messiah, but in other passages it describes Jesus as God's Son in a sense we can only call "unique" or "unshared":

"He who did not spare his own Son" (Rom. 8.32).
"But when the time had fully come, God sent forth his Son" (Gal. 4.4).
"Sending his own Son in the likeness of sinful flesh" (Rom. 8.3).
"He has . . . transferred us into the kingdom of the Son of his love" (Col. 1.13).

For the rest, Paul names Christ "the wisdom" of God

(I Cor. 1.24, 30, *cf.* Col. 1.15–17); "the Lord of glory" (I Cor. 2.8); and "the last Adam" (I Cor. 15.45ff., Rom. 5.12–21), i.e. the Founder and Inclusive Representative of the new humanity as the first Adam was of the old.

These titles (and the list is not exhaustive) show how St. Paul ransacked language and thought, to express the absolute significance of Jesus Christ. His Christology is simply a recognition of that rank in the world of being he was compelled to give to one in whom he had experienced the saving power of God himself. In Christ he had found "unsearchable riches". Through him he had gained access to the Father (Eph. 2.18). In his face he had seen shining the splendour of the Creator of all things (II Cor. 4.6). What wonder then if he believed that Christ's story did not start in a Bethlehem cradle, and that he saw the world and history as moving on to Christ?

We Christians in this twentieth century, whose mental world is so different from Paul's, cannot use all Paul's language when we proclaim Christ to men. Thought-forms have changed, and titles and concepts intelligible to Paul's contemporaries are alien and remote to our generation. Our task is, using the idioms and categories of our day, to assign to Christ the supreme place Paul gave him in the eternal purposes of God for us men and for our salvation:

> "For all things are yours . . .
> Whether the world, or life, or death,
> Or things present or things future,
> All are yours;
> But you are Christ's, and Christ is God's"
> (I Cor. 3.21–23).

Part Two

THE GOSPEL
ACCORDING TO ST. PAUL
FOR TODAY

Chapter One

OUR HUMAN PREDICAMENT

We have outlined the Gospel according to St. Paul. The question now before us is, What has this Christianity of his to say to us who live in other times and under other skies and are vexed by problems which never came within Paul's horizon? Can Paul speak to our condition, or is he just *ein antik denkender Mensch*—in plainer terms, an "old fogey" out of the Bible, an excellent man doubtless in his own day but hardly the man with the answers to the questions we are asking?

"Paul", says Karl Barth, "veritably speaks to all men of every age." Does he indeed? Certainly this is not the view of many of our contemporaries. For them, the very name of the apostle suggests the author of certain epistles "wherein are many things hard to be understood", who took a morbid interest in sin, was mightily exercised about the law of Moses and the Wrath of God, and had "a down on" marriage, women unveiled in churches and various other things.

Yet even those who dismiss St. Paul as "a Biblical antiquity" might sometimes stop to wonder why his Gospel has been "incomparably the greatest source of spiritual revivals in the Christian Church for nearly two thousand years".[1] If Paul is an extinct volcano, why has his message still power to warm men's hearts, as it warmed Wesley's in the eighteenth century and sent him through England like a lighted torch?

[1] Denney, *The Christian Doctrine of Reconciliation*, 179.

Why do our spiritual pulses still quicken and thrill at the mere reading of passages like Rom. 8 or I Cor. 13? Only flame can produce flame. Is it pure chance that Karl Barth, the man who started the theological revival in our time, found his delivering word in the Epistle to the Romans?

It will be our contention that it is no accident, that, if (to change our figure) the husk of Paul's Gospel is ancient, the kernel is instinct with fructifying life. Translate Paul's insights into modern terms, and they will come home again to the men of our day. After all, despite external changes, the human situation remains pretty much what it was in Paul's day. There seems not a little in our world to justify Frederick the Great's comment on the preacher who was descanting on the natural goodness of man: *Er kennt die verdammte Rasse nicht;*[1] and if Paul's description of our abiding human predicament should turn out to be accurate, we may also find that his remedy for it is no antiquated specific but, as he himself said, "a divine force for saving men".

I. ST. PAUL'S DOCTRINE OF SIN

Consider then, first, what I have called "our abiding human predicament". "'Tis the faith", says Browning,[2]

> *'Tis the faith that launched point blank her dart*
> *At the head of a lie—taught original Sin,*
> *The corruption of man's heart.*

Down nineteen centuries the Church's teaching—with, of course, from time to time, protests from Pelagius and others asserting that man need not sin—has been founded on what St. Paul taught about man's condition before God.

---

[1] "He doesn't know the perishing human race."
[2] *Gold Hair.*

Man is a sinner. He breaks God's law, not involuntarily merely but inveterately and inevitably, so incurring the divine condemnation. Let us try to set down succinctly what may be called Paul's doctrine of sin, remembering always that his doctrine is profoundly, even passionately, experimental.

First, we are "sold under sin". Sin, like slavery, is a *state* —not simply an incident without antecedents and consequents. It is a radical wrongness in our life, a turning away from the one true and righteous God, a depravity. This Sin, which Paul often personifies as if it were an independent Power, finds its base and stronghold in "the flesh" which is the material which gives sin its chance, our corrupt human nature, man's constitution as poisoned and fallen away from God.

Second, "there is none that doeth good". Sin is a *universal* state, something which affects every son of Adam. More, it is a corporate wrongness: like runners in the strawberry-bed, we are all connected up through a common life-root, and through that root-system flows evil.

Third, "the power of sin is the law". Sin is a violation of God's law—and that means not only the law of Moses but that bigger thing, the universal and eternal law of God, of which the Mosaic law is a form: a law written not merely once for Jews on tablets of stone (or scribal parchments) but written in the hearts and consciences of men the world over. "Through the law", Paul says, "comes the knowledge of sin." God's law shows up sin as sin—shows the sinner that his life is wrong with God—not only so, but it actually provokes to sin.[1] When the law says "Thou shalt not," man says, "I will." Further, "the law produces wrath"—God's

[1] A little American girl (reported by H. H. Asquith) said of the Ten Commandments: "They don't tell you what you ought to do, and they just put ideas into your head."

wrath, his holy love reacting against evil—the "adverse wind" of the divine will blowing against the sinner, not only at Judgment Day but now, and resulting in the degeneration and debasement of the sinner. And "the wages of sin is death". Sin, if persisted in, finally proves fatal.

Fourth, for our sin we men are "accountable to God", as morally responsible beings, made in God's image. Yet "by works of law shall no flesh be justified". No *tour de force* of human effort can save us from our sin and put us right with God. For man as sinner, no human cure is in sight. For the unrighteousness of man only a *divine* righteousness—if by God's grace there were such a thing—will avail as remedy.

Such is Paul's picture of "our human predicament". Here is no sky-blue anthropology, no doctrine of man's natural and congenital goodness. A sombre picture no doubt, but is it relevant, and is it true? Is not modern man justified in dismissing most of this as "the delusion of the synagogue" or the morbid vapourings of a pathological introvert of the first century? Some grain of truth we may allow to be present in it—we know, for example, that the instinctive revolt against a law which imposes itself on our nature is not something peculiarly Jewish but something universal and human.[1] Our twentieth-century psychologists can tell us much about that, though they can teach St. Augustine nothing about it.

Yet still the doubt asserts itself that most of it is hopelessly out of date, that original sin as Paul taught it is bound up with belief in the "fall" of a historical first man called Adam, and that "the wrath of God" is the figment of a mind which had not yet purged itself completely of sub-Christian views of God. Paul, after all, was very much a man of his time— a first-century Jew who had had a very unusual religious

[1] "Gainsay", says one of Mary Webb's characters, "and the blood's on fire."

experience; he had never heard of Darwin or Freud; he knew nothing of the modern scientific doctrine of heredity, and "repressions" and "complexes" are terms completely alien to his vocabulary. How can a modern Christian, who values his intellectual integrity, take Paul's picture of our spiritual predicament as true? True, we may translate some of his concepts into modern terms—interpret, for example, "the flesh" as the sum of the racial instincts we derive from heredity and environment, and so on. But can we, knowing what we do nowadays, accept in its broad outlines Paul's diagnosis of our moral and spiritual malady?

2. IS PAUL'S DIAGNOSIS TRUE AND TENABLE TODAY?

As men who (in Niebuhr's phrase[1]) "take the Bible seriously but not literally", I think we may hold, to begin with, that it is not necessary to accept every part of Paul's account of sin—its origin and its consequences—to maintain that his diagnosis is true. Thus, we are not bound to believe with Paul—if that is indeed his belief—that the sinfulness of all men stems from Adam's first act of disobedience. On the contrary, where the origin of sin is concerned, we may be content to avow ourselves agnostics. "It is no more necessary", says Denney, "in connexion with the Atonement, than in any other connexion that we should have a doctrine of the origin of sin. We do not know its origin, we only know that it is here."[2] Likewise, we may dare to question the connexion Paul makes between sin and death, finding in death the debt of nature rather than "the sacrament of sin". But the main question before us is this: Is Paul's picture of man as a sinner exposed to the divine condemnation and unable to save himself essentially

[1] *Christian Faith and Social Action*, 18.
[2] *Expositor*, Sept., 1903, 169.

true and tenable by us? Or must we consent with many moderns that what Paul calls sin is fundamentally ignorance, to be cured by education, or acquisitiveness—the Communist view—to be cured by the abolition of private property, or good in disguise, the soul's "growing pains", to be remedied by wise doses of "sweetness and light" as, under the guidance of our idealist philosophers, we move forward to perfection?

Obviously no purpose would be served by enlarging on Paul's remedy for sin, if in fact the disease no longer existed, had been cured, or else shown to be mere illusion—a piece of spiritual hypochondria. Paul no doubt held man to be inherently sinful. But nineteen centuries have passed, and in that time what progress man has made! If we could affirm that advancing civilization, the march of science, the discoveries of the psychologists had completely changed the human situation since Paul's day, delivering man from his ancient enemies, and making him master where once he had been slave, we might argue that since Paul's diagnosis was mistaken, his remedy was otiose and irrelevant. But can we? If we could convince ourselves that evil was due simply to external causes, or was a mere negation, "a not-yet"—a "hang-over" from our animal ancestry, humanity's growing pains, call it what you will—destined to pass away as the evolutionary process bore man onward and upward; or that higher education and improved psychological techniques would deliver man from his ignorance, correct his maladjustments, dispel his guilt complexes and, in short, turn bad men into good men, then we might dispense with St. Paul as we dispense with the doctor when the patient is obviously well set on the high road to good health. But the question is, Does an honest look at mankind today warrant such a confidence?

At the middle of the twentieth century we are much more disposed to listen to St. Paul than we were at its beginning. The "view from 1900" has been aptly summed up by an American writer[1]:

"The world looked forward to the twentieth century with a degree of confidence unequalled by any previous age and unregained since. Paced fast and slow, progress was sure, limitless, irreversible. Virtue walked with progress; they fed each other. The mood of the hour seemed to wipe out the black misery of preceding centuries. The worst was over; man was out of the woods."

The optimism of that time was, of course, founded on a very un-biblical, un-Pauline view of evil. Fifty to a hundred years ago we had almost persuaded ourselves that man was fundamentally good and that sin was the stock-in-trade of a morbid theology ("clerical crape-hanging") or the delusion of the synagogue (as the Nazis later named it). Those were the days when Hegel had persuaded many to see sin as "the emergence of man from the innocency of nature and a prelude to virtue"; when Walt Whitman announced his preference for the animals because they did not "whine about their condition"; and when men had come round to thinking that the existence of sin, so far as it was real at all, was a misfortune for which God was as much responsible as man. It was not surprising that even Christian people, catching the *Zeitgeist*, had decided (as Renan did) that St. Paul was "a back number" and put their trust in a God without wrath who brings men without sin into a kingdom without judgment through the ministrations of a Christ without a Cross.[2] 'God is not mocked", says Paul; but the men of that day

---

[1] Quoted in *Christian Faith and Social Action*, 24.
[2] Niebuhr, *The Kingdom of God in America*, 193.

little guessed how soon the wrath of God was to be revealed from heaven against the unrighteousness of men.

All this is changed. To all such bland optimism we have said a long good-bye. By the two colossal disasters of our time and their awful aftermaths we have learned, in blood and tears, "of what strange and terrible elements the world is made, and how dread a laboratory of good and evil is the heart of man".[1] The notion that evil is something superficial and external, clinging to man's heart as the barnacles to the ship's hull, is exploded. Discredited too is religious moralism's idea of sin as something merely incidental, a wrong choice, a not-now. We have returned to the older—the biblical—insight that man does evil because he is evil, that sin is something endemic in the human heart.

The case of the late Dr. C. E. M. Joad is typical of many. Having as a young man unquestioningly accepted Herbert Spencer's gospel of evolutionary optimism and trusted to science and psychology to usher in a brave new world, he was forced (as he told us in his last book, *The Recovery of Belief*) by the bitter logic of experience to admit that the Christian account of evil and sin is a pretty accurate appraisal of the human situation, and to avow that Paul of Tarsus is a better diagnostician of a man's state and prospects than Herbert Spencer.

3. THE DIMENSION OF THE DEMONIC

But (someone may say) St. Paul believed not merely in sin but in devils. Does he not talk freely of Satanic agency in human affairs? Does he not say that our "wrestling" is not merely with human adversaries but with "principalities and powers"? Does he not write as if there were "war in heaven" and God in Christ battling with superhuman

[1] N. S. Talbot (prophetically) in *Foundations* (1912), 18.

enemies? Does not, in short, the dimension of the demonic play a large part in his theology, and how can we accept it when Freud and his friends have explained all our deeds of darkness in terms of complexes, neuroses and the like? Here surely Paul was a man of his time. We have no need today of the hypothesis of the demonic. Or—haven't we?

The devil, it has been said, never did a better stroke than when he persuaded men to disbelieve in him. Can we be sure that even here St. Paul was mistaken? Can we so easily write off his belief in demonic agency as a first-century superstition unworthy of the credence of modern man? Our Lord, let us remember, shared this belief. So have many missionaries who have worked among primitive peoples. So do many modern thinkers and theologians—Otto Piper, Paul Tillich, C. S. Lewis, to name only three—not lightly to be labelled obscurantists or charged with fundamentalism.[1] It is the cosmic range and the sheer malignity of the evil they have seen in our world which have led them to re-espouse the Pauline view. Some of us, perhaps, have known a saintly soul pure, charitable, affectionate, who, when the reason went, became the awful opposite—foul, restless, wicked. We have said, "That horrible and inexplicable change is bad enough for the devil's work". And when we see, as we have seen in our time, a like awful change happening on an incomparably greater scale—insensate madness taking complete possession of a great and cultured nation and issuing in unspeakable horrors and cruelties—can we wonder that thoughtful men draw the Pauline conclusion? Nor must we imagine that Nazi Germany alone supplies the evidence.

[1] There is no metaphysical reason why the cosmos should not contain spirits higher than man who have made evil their good, who are ill-disposed to the human race, and whose activities are co-ordinated by a master-strategist.

"Necessity, expediency, defensible strategy," says J. S. Stewart, "we heard all those pleas in the days of Hiroshima and Nagasaki. But when men and nations of decent average morality are caught up and involved in such a situation, driven by an almost irresistible compulsion in directions in which they have no desire to go—'another law in my members, warring against the law of my mind'—who can doubt that something living and demonic is at work?"[1]

To borrow an analogy: There are times when the police lay their hands on a criminal, and yet are not satisfied. Behind this petty thief or thug is some other person, dimly guessed at, some master hand moving the pawn. The police can recognize that other's strategy, for the man in their hands could never have thought it all out by himself. The parable is obvious. The marks of Satan-like strategy in our world have moved many to Paul's view that more than human agents are pitted against us in the battle, that "the Power of darkness" is more than an outworn figure of speech, and that, though as Luther said, "his doom is writ", he still contrives to bedevil the affairs of men and nations.

4. MODERN MAN AND ORIGINAL SIN

It is time to sum up. Whatever view we may take of the demonic—and there is bound to be much disagreement among Christians—we have, one and all, learned the utter inadequacy of the views of evil we once held. When Bernard Shaw diagnoses it as the by-product of poverty, or the psychologist puts it down to the thwarted *libido*, or the evolutionist dismisses it as a mere imperfection, we may reply with St. Anselm, *"Nondum considerasti quanti ponderis sit peccatum."* There is a radical wrongness endemic in the very structure of our individual and corporate life, and judgment

[1] *A Faith to Proclaim*, 89.

—what Paul calls the Wrath of God, his holy love reacting against evil—falls inexorably on all who forsake the living God to live according to the world in self-deifying pride and egoism.

The evils, then, of which Paul speaks are not strange to us (though they may sound so, since Paul speaks of them as personal realities and we tend to think of them abstractly). It follows that if we are to present Paul's Gospel to the man of today, we must begin with the reality of sin and the fact of a fallen world. "If a Pauline preacher in our own day", wrote Alexander Whyte, "would preach to all men's hearts the all-forgiving grace of God, he must first bring home to all men's consciences the all-condemning law of God; if he would offer aright the gift of God, he must charge home the wages of sin; ay, and that not in a large and general and rhetorical way, but in a close and a personal and a home-coming way."[1]

There speaks a great master in the cure of souls. There too lies one of our cardinal difficulties. Emil Brunner has said[2] that the doctrine of original sin is one of five things in the Christian faith which are scandals to modern man. The scandal has nothing to do with Gen. 3 and the attempt to take it as literal history. Unless we are invincible funda-mentalists, we know that Gen. 3 is properly to be regarded as "a true myth"—that, though Eden is on no map and Adam's fall fits no historical calendar, that chapter witnesses to a dimension of human experience as present now as at the dawn of history—in plain terms, we are fallen creatures, and the story of Adam and Eve is the story of you and me.

No, sin is a religious concept—it is crime and rebellion against God; and the trouble is that modern man, though he

---

[1] *James Fraser, Laird of Brea*, 67.
[2] *The Scandal of Christianity*, Ch. 3.

encounters it wherever he turns, does not recognize it as sin, either in himself or in others, because he has lost that awareness of the living and holy God which makes it sin: "Against thee, thee only, have I sinned, and done that which is evil in thy sight." So the man of today tends to dodge the responsibility for sin. He may lay the blame on corrupting institutions (which he believes he can remake) or on the confusions of ignorance (which higher education will cure) or on psychological factors (which better psychology will eliminate), not discerning that all these are but symptoms of that deeper disease which Paul called indwelling sin, the corruption of man's heart.

More than that, confronted and depressed by the omni-presence of evil, he is prone to turn nihilist and write off the world as a meaningless chaos.

If, then, with Paul we are to face men with the fact of sin, our aim should not be to deepen despair but to kindle hope. And as a pointer to the true way we may take Paul's famous verse: "Where sin abounded, grace did much more abound." We have to teach men that the world is not a nihilist's nightmare but God's cosmos into which alien and chaotic things have entered. We have to proclaim both God and his forgiveness—God, in order that men may see the nature of their sin as rebellion against his holy love; and forgiveness, that they may consciously accept responsibility for actual sin committed. Men today know only too well that the world is mysteriously and radically wrong. To enable them to see the true nature of their darkness, we must show them also the light—the light of God's grace, who was in Christ reconciling the world to himself:

A second Adam to the fight
And to the rescue came.

Note on "the Wrath of God"

Sixteen times in his letters Paul refers to the Wrath of God. Thrice he gives the phrase in full, but generally he speaks of "the Wrath". He says that God "shows" wrath, or that his wrath is being "revealed" against human sin. Sinners are "vessels" (or "children") of wrath. Judgment day is "the Day of Wrath", as Jesus is our "Deliverer from the Wrath to come".

This language repels many Christian people. They would fain hold that "anger in every shape and form is foreign to God".[1] They would like to interpret Paul's phrase in terms of some impersonal doctrine of retribution—the inevitable operation of the law of cause and effect in a moral world.

But the Bible does not take this way. No student of the prophets can doubt that the Wrath of God was for them a personal activity of God. Nor can we doubt that, though Jesus laid a new emphasis on the love of God, he found the divine reaction to evil an awful reality. The same is true of St. Paul and the other New Testament writers.

To be sure, Paul speaks often of "the Wrath" without naming God. Is this because he thinks of it impersonally? Is it not rather because he finds it unnecessary to say whose wrath it is? What then does he mean by it? Quite simply, God's holy displeasure at sin. It is the eternal reaction against evil without which God would not be the Moral Governor of the world. St. Paul thinks of it as both present and future. It is that divine aversion to evil, which, though active now, will reach its climax at the Judgment.

Loyalty to the Bible will not then allow us to jettison the doctrine. But when we think of it we can remember two things. First, God's wrath is not to be thought of in terms

[1] The phrase is Berdyaev's.

of sinful man's. It is not "the emotional reaction of an irritated self-concern". We must not picture God as a man who suddenly loses his temper and throws aside his love. Rather, if we use human analogies, should we think of that "righteous indignation" which a good man feels in the presence of stark evil—and multiply it by infinity. Second, only a sentimentalist theology will find God's wrath incompatible with his love. (The opposite of love is hate, not wrath.) We should rather conceive God's wrath as the obverse of his love—"the adverse wind", the antagonism of his holy love to all that is evil. (Luther called God's wrath his "strange work", as mercy was his "proper work".)

Paul found the wrath of God a reality in his day. When men rebel against God (he said) God "gives them up" to their sins—suffering of body, hardening of their hearts, the complete obfuscation of their spiritual faculties (Rom. 1.18–32). Has this ceased to be true in the middle of the twentieth century?

Chapter Two

THE WAY OF DELIVERANCE

I. THE WAY OF DELIVERANCE IN PAUL'S GOSPEL

Life is short [says the old evangelical jingle]

> *Life is short,*
> *Death is sure,*
> *Sin is the wound,*
> *Christ is the cure.*

St. Paul declares that the only cure for the sin of man is the grace of God in the Living Crucified. We cannot save ourselves; we cannot, of our own strength, break the octopus grip which indwelling sin lays upon us. We are guilty men at the bar of God, and no "works" of ours can avail to put us right with him. There is no road to innocence for the guilty. Man as sinner is separate from God.

But, says Paul, it pleased God of his grace to bridge the awful chasm between his holiness and human sin, and to blaze a trail where the sinner could not go. The Gospel proclaims God's forgiveness, a forgiveness grounded in the divine deed of the Cross. "God was in Christ reconciling the world to himself." "He has made peace by the blood of his cross." "Therefore being justified by faith we have peace with God through our Lord Jesus Christ."

Regarded otherwise—from the human angle—there can be no release, no deliverance, no real spiritual life for sinful

6

man unless he gets an initial assurance of an unchanging love of God deeper than his sin. This he gets at the Cross. "God shows his love for us, in that while we were yet sinners, Christ died for us." This assurance, this new start and status, this gift, free and undeserved, of a new possibility of life, Paul calls "redemption", "justification" and "reconciliation".[1] God, taking the gracious initiative, offers it to us in Christ; and as we accept it, in faith—which is the soul's glad and obedient "Yes" to God's offer—God delivers us, forgives us and sets us right with himself. The first and decisive step on the road to salvation has been taken.

2. IS THE WAY OUT OF DATE?

Let this summary suffice. The question is: Are these only the moribund catchwords of an antiquated soteriology? Or is the experience of which Paul speaks something still verifiable by us in the middle of this twentieth century?

Some there are who fear that the reconciling power which streamed from Christ in the first century may have faded and failed with the passing of the centuries. They feel that the thing—the experience—of which Paul writes with such moving power is tied to the historical Christ who stands at a far and ever-widening distance from us. This is because they forget the Holy Spirit whose role it is to "take of the things of Christ and show them unto us". The Christ of the first century—the Christ who called Peter in Galilee and "arrested" Paul on the Damascus Road—does not belong only to the past. He is the Eternal Contemporary. The Spirit of God makes him such, and it is not from Pales-

[1] Strictly speaking, "justification"—the gift of a new status—is the first stage of "reconciliation" which signifies "restoration to fellowship".

tine, or from the first century, but here and now he is to be known and his reconciling power experienced.

Another mistake men make is to suppose that the issue Paul so often discusses—salvation by faith or by works—is a first-century issue, now as dead as the dodo. Let us admit that Paul's language has an old-fashioned sound, but not for the moment must we suppose that men rely no longer on "works". "When I was a student", writes Campbell Moody, "it seemed to me impossible that the errors of legalism, so thoroughly exposed by Paul, could still survive. By and by I found, in conversation with men both in Christian and in heathen lands, how much I was mistaken. Everywhere men seek, as of old, to satisfy their conscience by the performance of duty, or by telling themselves that they have done their duty, or that, at least, they are as good as those who make a profession of religion, and better, perhaps, for they are not hypocrites."[1]

Is not this, basically, the same delusion which Paul had to explode nineteen hundred years ago? Does anything so shut men out from the appeal of the divine love in the Gospel as self-justification? There are men and women in every congregation in that condition. Tell them that God is gracious, speak to them of his forgiveness and reconciliation in Christ, and they hear without real understanding, persuaded in their hearts that they have no need to repent and be forgiven. Only when they learn how insufficient is all their boasted goodness—only when they become so dissatisfied not with this or that fault in their lives but with their whole character, that they are ready to cry "God be merciful to me a sinner"—will they begin to realize that the Gospel speaks to their condition, and offers them the remedy they need. .

The Purpose of Jesus, 141f.

There is a passage in Denney's *Christian Doctrine of Reconciliation*[1] which goes to the very heart of modern man's complaint that he cannot assimilate Paul's teaching:

"There have always been people", he writes, "who found Paul intelligible and accepted the Gospel as he preached it. There are such people still, if not in theological class rooms, then in mission halls, at street corners, in lonely rooms. It is not historical scholarship which is wanted for the understanding of him, and neither is it the insight of genius: *it is despair*. Paul did not preach for scholars, not even for philosophers; he preached for sinners. He had no gospel except for men whose mouths were stopped, and who were standing condemned at the bar of God. They understood him, and they find him eminently intelligible still. When a man has the simplicity to say with Dr. Chalmers, 'What could I do if God did not justify the ungodly?' he has the key to the Pauline gospel of reconciliation in his hand."

These are telling words. Not to "the wise and the prudent"—to sophisticated modern men confident that they can save themselves by one technique or another—but to the "babes"—to the men who know what "despair" means and are marked by a great "simplicity"—does God reveal the deep secret of his grace in Christ. It was true then. It has never ceased to be true. It is true still.

But, indeed, to say that the deliverance which Paul describes is alien and unintelligible is to fly in the face of Christian testimony down many centuries. The discovery which "Christian" made that when he come up with the Cross the burden of his sins fell off his back and rolled into the empty sepulchre to be seen no more, while he went on his way rejoicing, "He hath given me rest by his sorrow and life by his death"—this discovery has been authenticated

[1] p. 180.

in every corner of the world by people of all classes. What Cornish miners and Kingswood colliers testified in the eighteenth century—

> *He breaks the power of cancelled sin,*
> *He sets the prisoner free—*

has been found true by thousands who have made the experiment. Countless people strike hands with Augustine and Bunyan, with Cowper and Newton, with Thomas Chalmers and James Smetham, when they tell how in their need and sin and despair they found deliverance in what St. Paul calls justification, by grace, through faith in Christ. Whatever in Paul is antiquated, remote, unrealizable, this article in his Christianity is not.

3. THE COMMUNICATION OF THE GOSPEL

Here, however, we encounter what is commonly called nowadays "the problem of communication". How are we to bring Paul's truth home to our contemporaries? The people to whom we speak, exposed as they are to the pressures of the age, find Paul's categories and thought-forms strange and remote. We shall certainly not "register" with many puzzled people in our congregations if we start talking about "the biblical paradox of man's radical sinfulness in the context of redeeming grace". The very word "grace" falls strangely on the ears of a generation to whom "Genesis is a biological term and Revelation the name of a suit-case".[1] And what does the man in the street, or even the man in the pew, make of words like "redemption" and "justification"? One is a metaphor from the slave-market; the other comes from the law court. When Paul told his converts they were

[1] D. H. C. Read, *The Problem of Communication*, 86.

"redeemed" by Christ's sacrifice, he was employing a metaphor which spoke to them with vivid power, for "redemption" from slavery was a familiar, everyday process in their world. To the men of our day, I fear, it is a clerical cliché full of holy sound and suggestion but signifying very little. Nor is the word "justification" any more luminous. Not only does it *not* explain itself, but long controversy between Protestant and Roman has confused its meaning. What to do about it is a very difficult question, worth much pondering. For the word, as Paul uses it, embodies a deep evangelical truth—a truth, moreover, which this generation badly needs to hear. "Justification" poses, in one word, the problem created by the holiness of God and the sinfulness of man. How is a sinner to secure that right standing with God which is necessary if he is ever to find communion with God and salvation? Many Christians in our day never even glimpse the problem, because they hold shallow views of sin, and because they cherish a sentimental, un-biblical conception of God, imagining him a complacent and easy-going Deity, with whom fellowship is a simple relationship, to be "taken in hand whenever we please and on no onerous conditions".[1] So they compromise the moral foundations of theology, and miss the profound truth which "justification by faith" expressed for St. Paul.

Only those whom God can regard as in some sense righteous are fit to be in fellowship with him. Yet, since "there is none righteous, no, not one", how can man ever hope to secure that right standing with God which he needs? This is the problem to which (Paul says) we have the divine solution in Christ. For it is the heart of the Gospel that God makes that right standing available, on the sole condition of man's faith, through the redemptive work of Christ.

[1] V. Taylor, *Forgiveness and Reconciliation*, 79.

Our forefathers, whose theological systems we dismiss so light-heartedly as out of date, at least saw the human problem and understood the divine solution. And whatever word we may adopt to replace "justification", it is the duty of all who preach and teach the Gospel today to emphasize the truth for which it stands.

Happily, Paul's third term "reconciliation" does not raise such problems of communication. It has two clear advantages: first, it states the whole problem in the language of personal relations—a language which never grows out of date: and, second, it answers to a universal need, for reconciliation to reality—however it be conceived—is something elemental for which all men crave, something which finds expression in all the great writers of the world, from Lucretius and Virgil to Goethe and Wordsworth.

It may be suggested, then, that the language of the home will move the men of our day when the language of the slave-market or even the law court leaves them cold. And have we not the best warrant in the world for employing it? May not the greatest of our Lord's parables serve as guide? What is the doctrine of the parable of the Prodigal Son if it is not the doctrine of God who "justifies the ungodly"? The Prodigal was made right with his father, absolutely right, not by anything he achieved, but simply by repentance and trust in his father's forgiving love.[1]

---

[1] Some people, who dislike the "Pauline" idea of mediation in forgiveness, point out that the parable of the Prodigal Son has no atonement in it. It is fair to reply that (*a*) there is no Christ in the parable either, (*b*) a parable makes one main point, and the atonement is concerned with a different point—not the freeness of the divine pardon but its cost, and (*c*) any proper doctrine of atonement must be based not on a single parable but on the whole set of facts presented in the life and teaching, death and resurrection of Jesus and in the experience of Christians.

Surely it is in such moving human terms that we should set forth the truth of reconciliation today. Men are in the plight of the Prodigal—alienated by their sin and guilt from the All-Father. This is the first thing they must learn, and they can learn it only through a "despair" like the Prodigal's. But such despair is the proper soil for the good seed of the Gospel. Then they must hear "the old, old story" proclaimed with all the relevance and modernity we can command—that the Father has given his only Son to deal finally with their sin and guilt, and that all that is necessary is repentance and the decision of faith. If we do this, men will see the possibility of a fresh start, of a new beginning, and by God's grace they may grasp it and make it their own.

4. THE PREACHING OF THE CROSS

All this involves preaching the Cross as Paul did, viz. as the place *par excellence* where God's forgiveness is made available for sinners. A Gospel which left out the Cross, or gave it only a minor place, would have seemed to St. Paul no Gospel at all. That "Christ died for our sins according to the scriptures," was the first article in Paul's *kērygma*, as it was in the *kērygma* of all the Apostles (I Cor. 15.1–11).

But can we proclaim "Christ and him crucified" to the men of our day as Paul proclaimed him to his contemporaries? We are told[1] that the modern man finds "the Pauline idea" of the Cross "scandalous" because, with the widespread depersonalization of human life and relationships in our time, he has no sense of guilt and recoils from the very notion of "the wrath of God" (i.e. a Holy Love in ceaseless and omnipresent reaction against evil in every shape and form).

[1] See Brunner, *The Scandal of Christianity*, 73f.

No doubt the temper of our age confronts the preacher of the Cross with a hard problem. Jowett of Balliol said once we were asking a great deal of men when we invited them to accept as the secret of the universe a Man who was hanged. To an age which worships power and whose symbol is the atom bomb, it can never be easy to proclaim a crucified Man as the place where God is seen putting forth his power to solve the hardest problem of all—the problem of setting bad men on the road to goodness and the Way Everlasting.

Yet, for our comforting, we may remind ourselves that even in Paul's day the Cross was a "scandal"; that, looking back over nineteen centuries, no single event in history can compare in power for good with the power of Christ crucified; and that, however unpropitious be the *Zeitgeist*, however inadequate our proclamation, "the Word of the Cross" has still that in itself which arrests and enthrals and subdues. Deep down in them the "depersonalized" men of our time, their own lives torn and crucified by tragedy and catastrophe, feel not only a kinship with "the Strange Man on his Cross" but a sense that here, at Calvary, they are dealing not with clerical clichés or fine-spun theological theorems, but with fact—with reality. May we not find here our point of contact and opportunity for leading men more deeply into the mystery of that act in which God in Christ "took the responsibility of evil upon himself and somehow subsumed evil under good"?[1]

Broadly speaking, men have seen the Cross in three ways: as Revelation, as Victory and as Expiatory Sacrifice. Each view has its truth; but none—nor all of them together—exhausts the total truth of the Atonement; nor does a man's salvation depend upon his acceptance of a particular theory. Nevertheless, it is worth while asking how Paul sees the

[1] *Letters of Principal James Denney to his Family and Friends*, 187.

Cross, if only to discover where a Pauline preacher will lay the emphasis today.

The first view we normally link with the name of Abelard. Its basic idea is that Christ on his Cross supremely reveals the suffering love of God in conflict with human sin, and by that revelation moves the hearts of sinful men to repentance. In her novel about Abelard, Helen Waddell has movingly set it forth. Abelard and his friend Thibault find a little rabbit crushed in a trap. Abelard breaks out to his friend, "Do you think there's a God at all?" "I know", replies Thibault, "only—I think God is in it too." "In it? Do you mean it makes him suffer too? You mean Calvary?" "Yes, but that was only a piece of it—the piece we saw—in time. Like that." Thibault pointed to a fallen tree, sawn through the middle. "That dark ring there, it goes up and down the whole tree. But we only see where it is cut across."

Did Paul ever see the Cross like that? I think he did. The man who wrote Rom. 8.32 certainly saw that everything in our redemption goes back ultimately to the self-sacrifice of God. And we too, who are called to preach the Cross, must see it as revelatory—the revelation at once of the sin of man and the love of God. Yet I am equally sure that a Pauline preacher must see a good deal more in it than this.

The second view is that which we associate with the name of Aulén in his book *Christus Victor*. Its cardinal idea is that Christ in his ministry and supremely on the Cross raided the dark empire of evil, vanquished the devil, and led captivity captive. The Cross is imaged as Christ's death-grapple with Satan, a conflict through which he emerges victorious by the Resurrection. Paul saw the Cross in this light too. It was of the Cross he was thinking when he wrote, "He disarmed the principalities and powers and made a public example of them, triumphing over them in him (or 'in it', i.e. the Cross)" (Col. 2.15). In days like these when the racial and cosmic nature of evil has led many to a revived belief in the reality of the demonic, this too is a note we may also strike in our preaching.[1] Martin Luther knew how to strike it, as witness his great hymn *Ein' feste Burg*, and in our own day Otto Piper, Paul Tillich, Oscar Cullmann, James S. Stewart and others have insisted that it must be struck anew.

Nevertheless, if I understand St. Paul aright, it is the third view of the Cross—the view which sees the death of Christ as an expiatory sacrifice for sin—which dominates Paul's thought. It seems to me, indeed, that to do justice to his view, we must also include in it those elements of truth for which the old "juridical" theory of the Atonement stood.

Nowadays we fight shy of the phrase "Penal Substitution", because too often in the past men presented it in crude, unethical ways. No doubt, too, Paul never calls Christ our "substitute" (though those who point out that the preposition he uses for Christ's work is *hyper*, not *anti*, forget Winer's dictum that "in most cases one who acts on behalf of another takes his place"); and the word "representative" is probably the better one to use. But the older commentators did not misconceive Paul's teaching altogether; and the truth which the old theory of the Atonement conserves is deeply rooted in Paul's classical statements about the Atonement (Rom. 3.25, Gal. 3.13 and above all II Cor. 5.21). "For our sake", Paul declares, "God made him to be sin for us who knew no sin, so that in him we might become the righteousness of God." What else can this mean but that the Cross is a divine deed wherein, by God's appointing, our condemnation came upon the sinless Christ, that for us

[1] The question is: How are we to preach it to a generation which has given up believing in the Devil?

there might be condemnation no more? The "penal" element in that statement is not to be eliminated by any exegetical legerdemain, and no doctrine of the Cross which rejects it can claim to be truly Pauline. Of course, we must always carefully define which we mean by the word "penal". We may never say that Christ's suffering was "penal" in the sense that it came upon him through a bad conscience or in the sense that the only Son of God's love was the personal object of divine anger. But, for Paul, Christ's suffering was certainly "penal" in the sense that he had to realize to the full the divine reaction against sin in the human race in which he was incorporated, and to which he had betrothed himself for better, for worse. If he had not done this, could he have been the Saviour of the race from sin or the Reconciler of sinful men to God?

"God forbid that I should glory save in the cross of our Lord Jesus Christ." Paul's glorying must be ours, though it be "foolishness" to the Greeks of our day. Do we find a full rationale of the Cross hard, nay impossible, to come by? Then let us not be discouraged. Others have found it so before us. Whatever we do, we must not scale down the Cross or offer men timid and half-hearted affirmations about it. Granted that an aura of ultimate mystery must ever encompass Calvary; granted that none of us may ever fathom all its depths or heights. On us lies the obligation to set it forth, using all the light God gives us. Surely it is better, with a bold and daring faith, to hold fast this towering Gospel truth in all its mystery than to traffic in pale and pithless platitudes about it, which never yet brought rescue and comfort to any soul in despair? Preach the Cross we must *eukairōs akairōs*. For by such things sinful men live, and wholly therein is the life of their spirit. Though they outgo us, their very immensity assures us that God is in them. For in such themes, however fumblingly we proclaim them, lies a Gospel big enough to meet the needs of a fallen world, and there only, as all the saints have witnessed, lies the secret of victorious Christian living:

> *I asked them whence their victory came.*
> *They, with united breath,*
> *Ascribed their conquest to the Lamb,*
> *Their triumph to his death.*

Chapter Three

NEWNESS OF LIFE
(1) FELLOWSHIP WITH CHRIST

The story goes that a Salvation Army lass once innocently accosted a famous bishop (was it Westcott?) expert in Greek tenses, with the question, "Are you saved?" To which the bishop is reported to have answered: "It depends what you mean. Do you mean *sōtheis*, *sesōsmenos*, or *sōzomenos*?"

Our concern in this chapter is with the third of these participles—with salvation as a present experience.

When a sinful man, by penitence and faith, has found pardon and acceptance with God through Christ, gaining at once a new status and a new start, he enters on what Paul calls *kainotēs zōēs*, life of a completely new kind and quality, the life of the New Order which Christ has brought. He enjoys an inner peace he had not known before; the Holy Spirit in his heart convinces him of his sonship to God; and an immortal hope—"the hope of glory"—is born in him. Not that he becomes suddenly and *per saltum* sinless (Paul was a realist, not a starry-eyed idealist). The old nature does not die so quickly as that. After all, the redeemed man is still "in the flesh" whose downward pulls and pressures will be with him, all the way, this side of eternity. "Not as though I were already perfect" (Phil. 3.12), said the Apostle looking at his own life, when he was a mature Christian; and we may be quite sure that what was true of Paul was true—

far, far truer—of all those ex-pagans in Corinth, Ephesus,
Philippi and Thessalonica whom Paul delights to dignify
with the name of "saints". *Simul justus et peccator* is Luther's
description of the new man, and complete sanctification is
still a long way off. Nevertheless, he has entered a new world,
the world of grace, and is potentially a new man, even if
many bits of the "old man" still cling to him (as Brunner
says somewhere) like bits of egg-shell to the young chick.
If he is not sinless, the power of his old master, Sin, has
been broken[1]; he has acquired a new Master, Christ, and is
now summoned, with the help of the Holy Spirit, to fight
the good fight against the world, the flesh and the devil.

Does all this sound to some like first-century theologiz-
ing, with no relation or relevancy to our life in the twentieth
century? Then try doing two things. First, try to read
Paul's essential thought out of its antique phrases into the
living language of today; and then having done that, look
into your own heart! Surely we who have had some
Christian experience can recognize the spiritual realities or
which Paul speaks—can testify not only (I hope) how hard
the "old man" dies but also how new in its essential
quality is that life which Christ has touched.

1. LIFE "IN COMMUNION WITH CHRIST"

This "newness of life", to which baptism is the door, is,
above all, a life "in Christ".

Whatever else it signified, life "in Christ" meant for St.
Paul life "in communion with Christ". St. Paul, as
Schweitzer has said, had grasped the fact that the essence or
being a Christian lies in the experience of being in fellowship with Christ—a Christ (let us add) no longer cramped

[1] On this point see Nygren, *Romans*, 240ff.

and constricted as in "the days of his flesh" but a Christ "let loose in the world", by the Resurrection, to become a ubiquitous and universal Personality. This experience of being in fellowship with Christ informs every letter Paul wrote: "If any one is in Christ," he says, "he is a new creation [or creature]" (II Cor. 5.17). "I am able for anything in him [Christ] who makes me strong" (Phil. 4.13). "Thanks be to God who in Christ always leads us in triumph" (II Cor. 2.14). And, at its deepest and richest, it is an experience of fellowship with Christ who died and rose, so that the believer lives, dies and rises with him into new life.

Of all this it has been said by a recent writer[1]: "The glory of the Pauline conception lies in just this, that the normal Christian in his normal life is 'in Christ'. To be 'in Christ' is not confined to a few people in moments of peculiar exaltation; it is ordinary Christian experience. Christianity transforms the ordinary. However freely the phrase is used, the reality to which it so succinctly refers is communion with Christ."

Here then (we may say) in fellowship with a living Lord we come on something fundamental—fundamental not only to Pauline but to all apostolic Christianity. "No apostle ever remembered Christ," it has been paradoxically put. For the first Christians the paramount miracle was Christ as a present power, not Christ as an admired person in history.

I wonder whether we Christians of the twentieth century make it basic today. Do we really understand what it means to believe in the Resurrection of Christ? "Look at the sequence," says James S. Stewart,[2] "risen from the dead, therefore alive for ever; therefore our contemporary; therefore able to confront us face to face." Do we fully realize

[1] A. Raymond George, *Communion with God in the New Testament*, 148.　　　　　　　　　　[2] *A Faith to Proclaim*, 153.

that in such communion with a contemporary Christ lies the true secret of the Christian life?

> *Shakespeare is dust, and will not come*
> *To question from his Avon tomb;*
> *And Socrates and Shelley keep*
> *An Attic and Italian sleep . . .*

> *They see not. But, O Christians who*
> *Throng Holborn and Fifth Avenue,*
> *May you not meet, in spite of death,*
> *A Traveller from Nazareth?*[1]

If this is not true, then Christianity is no more than an interesting exercise in religious antiquarianism, and Christ himself a

> *dead fact stranded on the shore*
> *Of the oblivious years.*

That it is true—that Jesus Christ is not merely a posthumous influence but a personal presence, is the testimony of Christian saints down nineteen centuries. Yet it is extraordinary how many of Christ's professed followers suppose that Christian discipleship means merely a harking back to the precepts and example of one who appeared suddenly upon the human scene nineteen hundred years ago, dazzled men with the brief splendour of his acts and utterances, and then vanished from it for ever.

That the Christian life finds its pattern in the example and teaching of Jesus, as recorded in the Gospels, is not in dispute; and Paul himself can speak of "fulfilling the law of Christ" and summon men to fashion their conduct "according to Christ". But the sovereign secret of living "according to Christ" and "fulfilling his law" is, as Paul well knew,

[1] John Drinkwater.

living with Christ—living daily in his fellowship and by his power. Is it not the secret still? "To be a Christian", said Phillips Brooks,[1] "is not merely to remember a departed Teacher and to try to remember his commandments, but to live with a living Friend, to gather out of his present life present warnings and inspirations, to let him guide us in all the little and great doings of our lives. Personal friendship with him is the soul of the Christian faith. It is the Christian faith."

If this is "mysticism"—though I suspect the more accurate phrase would be "I-and-Thou communion"—then every true Christian is a mystic. "*Secretum meum mihi*", the old mystics used to say: the Christian may say it too, for he will never be able to explain his experience fully to an outsider. Yet, however fitful and faint his sense of Christ's presence may be, the experience is real, past all gainsaying, whether the witness be borne by the Quaker J. G. Whittier:

> *And, warm, sweet, tender, even yet*
> *A present help is he;*

or by the Congregationalist Ray Palmer:

> *I see Thee not, I hear Thee not,*
> *Yet art Thou oft with me;*

or by the Roman Catholic Francis Thompson:

> *And lo, Christ walking on the water*
> *Not of Gennesaret, but Thames!*

Here then we are dealing not with something peculiar to Paul and the first century but with something *gemeinchrist-lich*, as the Germans say, and common to Christianity in any century: with something, or rather someone who joins

[1] *Christ the Life and the Light*, 104.

together in the communion of Saints Paul and Patrick, Samuel Rutherford and George Fox, David Livingstone and Charles Raven, and not these only but an innumerable multitude of men and women, unknown to fame or the history-books, who have walked through the bright and the dark places of this world companioned by an unseen Presence.

2. LIFE "IN THE COMMUNITY OF CHRIST"

But life "in Christ" meant also life "in the community of Christ". The phrase, as recent scholarship has shown, had clear corporate overtones. It connoted life in the Body of Christ, which is the Church. When Bultmann writes[1] " 'In Christ', so far from being a formula for mystic union, is primarily an ecclesiological formula", he is wrong in what he denies but right in what he affirms. "Christianity means Christ", we say often, and rightly; but Christ means the Church; and Paul would have found the greatest difficulty in comprehending a man who, claiming to be "in Christ", i.e. a Christian, declared "he had no use for the Church".

This is a truth which we Protestants who name Paul master in spiritual things, have not always remembered. Dr. Visser 't Hooft has charged nineteenth-century Protestants with failing to take seriously the doctrine of the Church. The nineteenth century was the heyday of evangelical individualism when even pious Christians might be heard to say, "Give us more Christianity and less Church-ianity". (In that heresy they were confirmed by many New Testament scholars with whom it had become a dogma of critical orthodoxy that Jesus never intended to found a new society like the Church.) The Bible might "know nothing of solitary religion", as the New Testament knows nothing of

[1] *The Theology of the New Testament*, I, 311.

"unattached Christians"; but some of our forefathers, by failing to grasp the centrality of the Church in New Testament religion, at least lent colour to the notion that the Church was an optional addendum to the soul's communion with its Lord.

We do not hear much of this language nowadays. We no longer regard Christian salvation as some purely isolated transaction between the sinner and his Saviour. The doctrine of the Church has become a hackneyed theme at conferences, and our theologians are now well aware that "no Christian doctrine can be satisfactorily stated in terms of the individual".

To be sure, the initial decision of faith is, and must ever be, an individual affair. Nothing can be so solitary and personal as God's call and the soul's answer to him. But when (to use the old phrase) a man "decides for Christ", he enters, willy-nilly, into what St. Paul calls "the Body of Christ". "We become related to Christ singly," writes Dr. John A. Mackay,[1] "but we cannot live 'in Christ' solitarily." In Paul's conception of Christianity the Church is not an option but a necessity: a *sine qua non*, not an extra.

To explore the contemporary relevances of all Paul's teaching about the Church is quite impossible here, even if I had the ability—which I have not—to make my way securely in waters where even stout theologians take many a buffeting and are sometimes like to sink. But let me raise three quite simple and obvious points.

The first concerns the nature of the Church. It involves the question Brunner has lately been asking very pertinently[2]: How stands the Church, regarded as a spiritual organism, as the Body of Christ, in relation to the institutions we call "churches" today? Which ought the Church

[1] *God's Order*, 117.   [2] In *The Misunderstanding of the Church.*

to be, primarily? Fellowship or institution? Can there be any doubt where the Pauline stress falls? For him, the Church is pre-eminently a fellowship, not an institution. It is a pure communion of persons united to Christ, its living Head, and to one another through the Holy Spirit: not a highly organized, legally administered institution.

"This is all very well," someone may reply, "but you are talking of the Church when it was very young. Nineteen centuries have supervened. Development was inevitable." We may admit this, but still wonder whether it is enough to plead in reply that, as Christianity moved out into the great pagan world and had to meet its challenges, it had to become organized and was bound to become an institution with laws of its own. Take the Church of Rome as the supreme example of a church which has become a great legal—even political—institution, and hear what Dr. Inge had to say about it:

"It is impossible to find any sanction in the New Testament for a militant political church. But the Catholic modernists argue that this development was inevitable; it was forced by circumstances on the Church which had to consolidate itself against persecution from without and against disruptive movements within. If Christ meant his Church to survive, they say, he could not have disapproved of the only policy which could ensure its survival. This, however, is a bad defence of an institution which claims to be divine. Force and fraud are not the weapons of the Holy Spirit."[1]

I submit that there is substance in this criticism; but if we leave the Church of Rome and look at our own "churches" today, are we never smitten with an awful sense of their unlikeness to the Body of Christ as Paul conceived it? Here

[1] *Vale*, 36.

surely Paul's teaching may serve still as a salutary reminder of what a *vera ecclesia* ought to be.

Consider, next, the perennial problem of our Christian disunion. "There is one Body", says St. Paul. For him, the one-ness of the Church is as axiomatic as the uniqueness of the Church's Lord. It is with sheer horror that he hears of the "parties" in Corinth, "Is Christ divided?" And we cannot doubt that if he were here today, he would condemn our ecclesiastical divisions as roundly as he condemned the cliques in Corinth. In our home churches, alas, we seem still able to view our disunity with some complacency. We comfort ourselves by saying that, in spite of all our denominations, we have a spiritual unity with Christians in other "churches", and we sing (God forgive us):

> *We are not divided,*
> *All one Body we.*

It is in the mission field that the scandal of our Christian divisions presses most heavily. Converts not unnaturally ask, "Why force your divisions on us? Why cannot we, in face of the pagan world, worship and evangelize and take the sacraments along with our friends?" There is no real answer to this question, certainly not the common Protestant plea: "Why worry about corporate reunion? Among all true Christians there exists already a unity of spirit." We recall how St. Paul dealt with the "spiritual" Christians in Corinth who were so proud of their possession of the Spirit that they forgot all need for corporate unity. When we look at our denominations and divisions today, in which one man says, "I am of Calvin", and another, "I am of Wesley", and a third (to name no more), "I am of Luther", can we not hear Paul, across the centuries, indignantly demanding, "Is Christ in fragments? Were we baptized into the name of John Calvin? Did we profess our faith in John Wesley? Do we pray to Martin Luther—or William Temple?" Surely it is a task laid upon the minds and hearts of all who call themselves Christians, of all who believe the great High Priestly Prayer to be a true mirror of the mind of Christ, to work and pray for the healing of the Broken Body of our Lord.

Or take, finally, the question, What is the true mission of the Church in the world? No worthier answer has been given than St. Paul gave in Ephesians, perhaps the most contemporary book in the New Testament.

In the forefront he sets the Body of Christ "the fullness of him who is being wholly filled". Christ and his Church, Head and Body, form a corporate Personality, and Christ is "filled" as the Body grows up into its full spiritual stature. The mission of this Church is to "gather into one all things" in Christ the cosmic Redeemer. Of this consummation the union of Jew and Gentile in a single divine community is the pledge. It is the divine will that the Church shall grow, healing the divisions of men and reconciling them to God and each other, till all is complete in "the Christ that is to be".

Such is Paul's vision, and he speaks with pointed directness to the men of our day, hungry for true community yet living a "barbed-wire" existence, constantly shadowed by the menace of the atom bomb. We have a long way to travel before that divine dream of Paul's comes true. Nevertheless, in spite of all our divisions, we see today an *Ecclesia* which is in a true sense world-wide. The mustard seed planted in Galilee and watered by the bloody sweat of the Saviour's Passion has become a great Tree. May its leaves be indeed for the healing of the nations!

3. LIFE IN KOINŌNIA

The new life "in Christ", then, is essentially life in community, or *koinōnia*. The word suggests the rite in which fellowship with Christ finds its focus and climax: the Lord's Supper. So we may round off this chapter with a word on St. Paul and the sacraments.

What importance did he attach to them? We pose the question because three or four decades ago when the Greek Mystery religions were exciting the scholars' interest, Reitzenstein, Lake and others gravely affirmed that St. Paul—long regarded as a pillar of Protestantism—was really the begetter of early Catholicism. This Catholicism (we were further told) was a sacramental cult bearing very strong resemblances to the Greek Mysteries with their *ex opere operato* sacraments. The inference was obvious: Paul had turned Christianity into a mystery religion.

The work of subsequent scholars, from Schweitzer to W. D. Davies, has shown this to be a libel on the Apostle. We cannot here go into their evidence and arguments. Suffice it to say that a man who goes out of his way to warn his converts, as Paul does in I Cor. 10, that the possession of sacraments confers no moral or spiritual security on them —a man who can write, "Christ did not send me to baptize but to preach the Gospel" (I Cor. 1.17)—can hardly be said to hold mystery religion views about the sacraments. Faith or sacraments? Which is the soteriological *sine qua non*? Paul, I am sure, would have heartily disliked this *Entweder-Oder*. But can any candid reader of his Epistles doubt that the Apostle deemed faith the one sufficient condition, on man's side, for receiving salvation?

On the other hand, the ultra-Protestant who regards the sacraments as merely acted parables of spiritual truths can hardly look to Paul for backing. The "realism" of Paul's language about baptism in Rom. 6 shows, in my judgment, that he thought of the rite in the same way as the Old Testament prophets thought of their symbolic actions. By the action the prophet conceived of himself as entering into the divine purpose and helping it forward. The act was an *arrabōn* of the total reality as yet incomplete: no bare symbol but an "effective sign" which, by the working of God's Spirit, could help to convey what it signified.

As for the Eucharist, I Cor. 10 shows that Paul regarded the Supper as "supernatural food and drink" because it mediated the closest conceivable communion between the living Crucified and his People.

A recent American judgment on the whole issue seems to me just:

"Paul", writes Professor Clarence T. Craig,[1] "ascribed no automatic virtue to the Lord's Supper any more than he did to baptism. Yet it is equally clear that he thought very realistically about the value of the community meal. It was no mere symbol but a very real partnership in which the bread and wine brought actual participation in all that the life and death of Christ had brought to men. It is useless to ask how far he anticipated later theories of the Church. But the Apostle certainly believed in a very real presence. The sacraments did not make faith unnecessary, but Paul would not have understood an expression of Christian faith apart from a community in which the Lord's Supper was celebrated."

By Pauline standards, therefore, not only Quaker attitudes to the sacraments but all mere "memorializing" views of the Lord's Supper are inadequate. What the real presence meant for him may be very hard to determine; but he

[1] *The Interpreter's Bible*, Vol. 10, 143.

certainly did not think of sacramental grace as a divine "stuff" secreted in the "elements", which acted on a man's soul as an aspirin acts on his body. For him, the sacraments drew their meaning from the redeeming *work* of Christ rather than from his *essence* and on man's side, faith was indispensable.

It is worth noting that in I Cor. 11 Paul relates the Supper to all three phases of salvation. The Supper looks back to Christ's finished work—"You proclaim the Lord's death". It is a communion with the living Christ who is host at his board. And it is a foretaste of perfected salvation—"till he come". I do not think the Apostle would have quarrelled with D. S. Cairns's[1] admirable summary of the Supper's significance—"a retrospect, and a prophecy, with a renewal of the Covenant face to face". In the Supper we look back to the night in which the Lord was "delivered up" for us men and for our salvation; we look forward to the time when "the whole human race will be home, gathered round the Father's table, after Iliads and Odysseys yet to be"; and we keep our tryst, in humble and adoring gratitude, with him who shed his blood for us, and who is present at his table, "unseen but not unknown", to communicate his saving self to us, as we accept him in the glad response of faith.

[1] D. S. Cairns: *An Autobiography*, 201.

Chapter Four

NEWNESS OF LIFE

(2) POWER AND PRINCIPLES

In our last chapter we described the new life of the Christian as life "in Christ"—a life at once "in communion with Christ" and "in the community of Christ".

But the half only has been told. If you set a man free from prison and require him to lead a new life, you must give him some idea of the new life expected of him and also some help to enable him to attain it. (*Kat' anthrōpon legō*, as Paul would say. I am using a human analogy to express a divine truth.) Both these things, according to St. Paul, God supplies to men in the Gospel. He gives them a pattern for life—it is to be *kata Christon*, "according to Christ" (a phrase to be studied presently)—and he equips them with power to achieve it. This power is what Paul calls "the power of the Holy Spirit" (Rom. 15.13, 19).

I. THE POWER OF THE NEW LIFE: THE HOLY SPIRIT

It has been said that if St. Luke had not left us a narrative of how the Holy Spirit descended on Christ's followers on the Day of Pentecost, we should have been under the necessity of conjecturing such an event. The Resurrection and Exaltation of Jesus do not adequately account for the Church. It is the gift of the Exalted Lord that alone explains it. The advent of the Holy Spirit is as much an event of history as the coming of Christ.

The Holy Spirit, then, is no private *theologoumenon* of St. Paul's. It was a gift of God which he shared with those who were "in Christ" before him. We are wont, however, to say that, whereas the earliest believers were prone to see the signs of the Spirit primarily in odd, abnormal phenomena like "speaking with tongues", Paul was the first to direct attention to those less spectacular fruits of the Spirit in heart and life, like *Agapē*, which were apt to get misprized and slighted. But we may well be mistaken. Conceivably the Apostle was teaching a lesson which was not new but had been forgotten or ignored.

What is not in dispute is the centrality of the Holy Spirit in the Gospel according to St. Paul. In only one Epistle—the brief letter to Philemon—does the Spirit fail to appear. In the others it is a case of *Circumspice*, and in his greatest chapters like Rom. 8 the Spirit dominates the scene. One might as well try to explain Paul's Christianity without the Spirit as modern civilization without electricity.

Let us refresh our memories with Paul's most characteristic teaching.

For St. Paul the Christian era is "the dispensation of the Spirit", the signs of which are "freedom", "power" and "joy". So he sets the Christian life—its beginning, its middle and its end—in the context of the Spirit. The condition of the Spirit's coming is "hearing (the Gospel) with faith", and at baptism upon conversion the believer receives the Spirit as an invisible "seal". The Church, Christ's Body, to which baptism is the door, is the sphere in which the Spirit does his quickening work.

All Christian skills are *charismata*, "grace-gifts" of the Spirit. All genuine Christian confession of one's faith, such as "Jesus is Lord", has its source in the Holy Spirit; and if we are sure of God's love to us declared in the Cross, it is because of the Spirit "flooding" our hearts. All true Christian prayer is "in the Spirit"—when we falter and fumble in our devotions, it is the Spirit who assists us, and when in filial intimacy we cry "Abba, Father", it is the Spirit assuring us we are sons of God. All authentic Christian behaviour is a "walking by the Spirit", as all lovely Christian virtues and graces—from "love" to "self-control" —are the Spirit's "fruit". When we fight the good fight against sin, the flesh and the devil, our ready and sufficient resource is the Spirit. And if we hope for a life as immortal as Christ's own, our hope rests in possessing the Spirit of him who raised Christ Jesus from the dead.

Nor is the Spirit some passive and impersonal influence operating in a soul-less, mechanical way. The Spirit is active, personal and purposive power working for Christlike ends, for the Spirit is "the Spirit of Christ" or "the Spirit of his Son". Consider how personal are the verbs used to describe the Spirit's work. The Spirit "leads", "testifies", "strengthens" and "sanctifies". Dwelling in human hearts, he "searches" and "reveals" divine secrets, and "intercedes" for us "according to the will of God." We may "grieve" the Spirit as we would a friend; we can "quench" his flame; but as we "set our mind on the Spirit", "live by the Spirit", are "aglow with the Spirit", we have freedom from the law, the secret of victorious living, and the "guarantee" (*arrabōn*) of everlasting life.

So rich, so deep, so wide is Paul's conception of the Spirit.

When we read his pages, so filled with an unearthly buoyancy, and, then, travelling down nineteen centuries, turn to survey the Christian scene today, have we not often felt (in Wordsworth's phrase) that somehow

> *there hath past away a glory from the earth?*

How little in evidence in our sedate and stuffy Christian society is that consciousness of indescribable richness and power which throbs through the apostolic records! Somehow the spiritual temperature has dropped; high poetry has become flat prose; and we feel that if Paul were to come among us today he might almost take us to be descendants of those disciples in Ephesus who had never heard there was such a thing as the Holy Spirit.

This is a mood of the soul to which the best of us are subject at times. But of course we are wrong. God does not go back on his gifts. The gift of Pentecost has not been withdrawn. The same Holy Spirit which in the first century wrought in Antioch, Ephesus, Corinth, Rome and wherever the Gospel "flew like hallowed fire from soul to soul" is still at work in our world today:

> *The centuries go gliding,*
> *But still we have abiding,*
> *With us that Spirit holy*
> *To make us brave and lowly.*

When that mood takes us, we need to recall our Lord's word to Nicodemus that the wind of the Divine Spirit "bloweth where it listeth". We cannot command it. There are tides of the Spirit, and we cannot tell why God seems to flood one generation or one part of the world with his power, while he seems to leave another like a piece of parched ground. But, second, when we are tempted to suppose that the Divine Power which Paul knew has gone from our world, it is because our vision is too narrow and confined, because we do not take a wide enough view of God's dealings with men in our time. We fail to remember "the great new fact" of our day—the existence of something like a world-wide Church resulting from the unparalleled missionary expansion of the last century and a half. We fail to remember the mighty chorus of Christian testimony that goes up now in every quarter of the globe, and that more men since 1918 have sealed their witness to the Faith with their life's blood than in all the persecutions of the Christian Church. We fail to remember the growing consciousness of the scandal of Christian disunity and the strong hunger among Christian men for a world community in Christ, of which the South India experiment and the Ecumenical Movement are happy first-fruits. We fail to remember the astonishing fertility of Christian thought in our day as evidenced, for example, in the theological revival of the last three decades. All this—and how much more—is proof that the Holy Spirit is moving mightily in our world no less than in St. Paul's.

Nevertheless, it must be admitted that for many Christians among us today Paul's teaching about the Spirit holds a great vagueness, and even unreality. They believe in God the Father; they believe in Christ the Son; but they have no vital conviction of the Spirit's reality and power. This failure of belief is often reflected in our observance of the great Christian Festivals. We make much of Christmas and Easter; we make very little of Whitsuntide. A hundred years ago F. D. Maurice wrote to his *fiancée*:

"I should like to be with you on Whit Sunday, but this year we must be content to wish each other the infinite blessings of it at a distance. They seem to me more wonderful the more I think of them. Sometimes it seems as if they were the root of all our life. I cannot but think that the reformation in our day, which I expect is to be more deep and searching then that of the sixteenth century, will turn upon the Spirit's presence and power."[1]

How many of us think that way—the Pauline way—about the Spirit? And may not our failure to believe in "the Spirit's presence and power" be part of the reason why the reformation and revival of true religion, for which we no less than Maurice yearn, is so long delayed?

I am not saying that much modern Christianity is consciously Binitarian; yet even in orthodox circles where belief in the Holy Spirit is an unquestioned article of faith, the conception of the Spirit's sphere of operation is sadly circumscribed. We think of the Spirit as the Illuminator in specifically sacred things; we do not think of him (as Paul did) as the Enabler of the whole Christian life; not only illuminating the mind and reason but searching down into the realm of the "paralogical" and "unconscious" and mobilizing all the hidden energies of the human spirit.

One reason for this is that in our rationalizing age we suspect people—as Bishop Butler suspected John Wesley—who "pretend to extraordinary manifestations of the Spirit". In many orthodox quarters the merest suggestion of being "aglow with the Spirit" is associated with "religious fanaticism or with the aberrations of sectarian groups that live upon the fringe of ecclesiastical Christianity". Another reason is that, bemused by a false scientific philosophy, we assume nature to be "a closed system" impervious to the invasion of any power coming, as the Germans say, *senkrecht von oben*.[2] And a third is undoubtedly just pure human sinful self-reliance—our bondage to "the flesh", as Paul would say—

---

[1] Quoted by Alec Vidler in *Christian Belief*, 55.
[2] So David Hume spoke scoffingly of "supposed illapses of the Spirit and inspiration from above".

which is not ready to let the strong Spirit of God have his
own sovereign way with us.

Such an attitude affects both thought and action. The
theologian who does not take the Spirit seriously (and
Brunner has called the Spirit "the theologian's stepchild")
finds a grave lacuna in his Christian thinking, a lacuna
which soon becomes a lacuna of action. The late Wheeler
Robinson[1] has told how, during a serious illness in 1913, he
was led to ask himself why the truth of evangelical Christianity which he had preached to others failed to comfort him
in his hour of need. Christian truth seemed to him like a
great balloon, with ample lifting power—if only one had
the strength to grasp the rope which trailed from it. In short,
his personal religion lacked vitality. Seeking what was lack-
ing, he found it in his neglect of the New Testament conception of the Spirit. The discovery revivified his own faith
and led him to the writing of his book on the Spirit which
has helped many.

Robinson's experience contains salutary warning, more
especially for us who are professionally concerned with
religion. Our very familiarity with sacred things may produce an atrophy of spiritual response. Like Father Hilary
in Rossetti's poem, we need, from time to time, to climb up
from the level of our professional duties to the roof of the
church where the winds of God are blowing, that we may
inhale

> *the breath*
> *Of God in man that warranteth*
> *The inmost utmost things.*

Constant returning to the great Pauline chapters on the
Spirit will help us to recover something of the lost secret;

[1] *The Christian Experience of the Holy Spirit*, 4.

for to keep the mind steadily on the subject is to open the way for ever-fresh experience. It has been said that whatever is not apostolic is not safe. If this is true, a returning to the ancient springs of power may be the most clamant need of our latter-day Christianity. "What will it profit us", asked George Fox once, "that we have the Scriptures, if we have lost the Spirit that wrote them?" Why should we not recover the faith that God the Holy Spirit can still work dynamically in the lives of men, piercing down to the deepest reaches of human personality and empowering them for the tasks of Christian living? When will we learn from St. Paul that the Gospel is not merely a divine message but "a divine force for saving men", that the power which he calls "the Spirit of God" has not petered out with the passage of the centuries but is still there for those who will receive it, and that the Church's true work can be done by no power or might of men but only by him whom the Creed calls "the Lord, the Life-giver".

2. THE PRINCIPLES OF THE NEW LIFE

From the power of the new life we turn now to consider its principles. For St. Paul, "truth was always truth in order to goodness". How does he conceive of the good life? What is his theory of it? What are its motives and standards? And how far are they valid for us?

Let us start with the theory. "Christian ethics", Brunner has said,[1] "is the science of human conduct as it is determined by divine conduct." Paul might not have put it that way, but he would not have quarrelled with the definition. The Christian way of life grows out of—is determined by— the Gospel. One is the root; the other is the fruit. It is not

[1] *The Divine Imperative*, 86.

good works that make a good man, but the good man—the man who has been transformed by God's saving action in Christ—who does good works. "The rose", says Weinel,[1] speaking of Paul's ethic, "asks not why. It blooms because it blooms. So is Christian morality, a morality which has overcome all legality."

Christian goodness, then (and this is our second point) is not legal. It is "grace" goodness, not "law" goodness. The Jew supposed that, to enjoy fellowship with God, he must first make himself a good man, and this he would do by keeping the law. Paul found that it did not work that way. He found that it was only by fellowship with God that he had any hope of becoming a good man. This fellowship God offered him in Christ. So he came to see that man's task is not to make himself good in order that God may accept him but to enjoy acceptance with God in order to be made good. All this finds terse expression in an old Puritan theological classic:

"Both these laws (the law of Moses and "the law of Christ") agree in saying, Do this. But there is this difference. The one says, Do this and live. The other says, Live and do this. The one says, Do this for life. The other says, Do this from life."[2]

We must, however, add that Paul knew very well that the Christian life is not so simple and spontaneous a thing as Weinel's metaphor about the rose suggests. Rather (and the proof is in the imperatives of Rom. 6) Paul saw the good life as both gift and task. God, having set a man right with himself and endowed him with the Spirit, then requires him to live as a new man should. He is to become, by divine grace, what he potentially is. If God is at work in him for

[1] *St. Paul, the Man and his Work*, 135.
[2] *The Marrow of Modern Divinity*.

his salvation, he is also summoned to work it out for himself.

All this is the heart of evangelical ethics, whether in the first century or the twentieth. Laws can point men to the good life, but they cannot make men good. What they cannot do is to "break the power of sin in the flesh"—or, as we might say, the downward pull of our inherited racial instincts. What is needed is the implanting of a new principle of life in us which will overcome the old nature and produce "the new man after Christ". And Christian goodness, now as then, should be the natural, inevitable unfolding of it in moral thought and action. It was said of a good Christian woman by an admiring neighbour, "She does good mechanical." So the Gospel should produce its fine moral fruits. Faith should flower in love, and goodness flow from the transformed man like water from a pellucid spring.

This is the spiritual theory of the matter; but we live in a fallen world, and St. Paul was too much of a realist ever to forget that he was dealing with very fallible men and women in whom the power of sin, though broken through their union with their new master Christ, was by no means dead. He realized too that if most of us are to walk the way of the good life we need signposts to help us forward—quite simple and plain signposts.

It is interesting to note therefore how much catechetical *"paraenesis"* [1] there is in his letters (see Gal. 5.13–6.10, Col. 3.1–4.6, I Thess. 4.1–12; 5.12–22): what might be called plain "Do this-es" for young converts who are not yet mature, not yet firm-set in the Christian way, not yet ready to rise to the full height of the Christian ethic. The morality of these sections has been much studied recently, and we know now that many of its maxims stemmed from

[1] "Moral instruction with a dash of exhortation."

pre-Christian roots, representing the best ethical teaching current in Hellenistic Judaism, and that it formed part of the minimum morality demanded of their converts not by Paul only but by all the apostolic missioners.

Exhortations to make a clean break with the bad old life and begin a clean new one; injunctions to honesty, purity, truthfulness, sober living and hard work; regulations for decent family life; advice about circumspect conduct towards outsiders, with a summons to respect the civil powers and pay all lawful taxes—this was the staple of it. Rather unexciting and pedestrian moral counsel, we may think; and yet we must not scorn it or deem it irrelevant in days like these when the old landmarks of morality are crumbling, family life is being undermined, and sexual laxity is rife. In a nominally Christian land it may be superfluous to tell catechumens not to provoke their pagan neighbours, but it is still necessary to tell those who "join the Church" that they are required to keep the elementary moral laws. If Paul found it necessary to order the Thessalonians to be honest and work hard, or the Romans to pay their taxes and use the civil authorities with respect, we may acknowledge his sound sense and take our cue from him. We have still, and—to judge from present prospects—are likely to have for a long time, many "babes in Christ" who must be fed on the milk of elementary morality before they can go on to the strong meat of the full Christian ethic.

From the Pauline theory of the good life let us turn to its pattern. This can be put in two words: it is to be *kata Christon*—"according to Christ" (Col. 2.8, II Cor. 11.17, etc.). Narrowly interpreted, this might mean "according to Christ's example and command"; but we may reasonably take it to describe all behaviour which derives its law and impulse from the whole new fact of Christ. It will then comprise all the distinctively Christian motives and principles of action.

In its most general form, it can be expressed: "Act in a manner befitting the Gospel of Christ." We might call this the *noblesse oblige* motive. It comes out clearly in sentences like, "Let your manner of life be worthy of the gospel of Christ" (Phil. 1.27), or "I beg you to lead a life worthy of your calling" (Eph. 4.1). Spiritual rank imposes moral obligations on us. It behoves us, as recipients of God's grace and mercy in Christ, to "live up to" our high calling.

Another such principle we might paraphrase as: "Act as members of Christ's Body." We may call this the *koinōnia* motive. "As you are really members of Christ's Body", Paul says in effect, "you must make your Christian behaviour conform accordingly. No Christian, remember, is an end in himself. He must always ask himself the question, Will my action build up or destroy the Body of Christ?" This is the principle of action Paul commends to the Corinthians worried about "meats offered to idols" and to the Romans who were discussing, on religious grounds, the rights and wrongs of vegetarianism; but it is a principle capable of wide application to the manifold problems which may vex our Christian fellowships today.

A third and important Pauline rule for Christian action is the one he gave the Galatians: "Fulfil the law of Christ" (Gal. 6.2). This is the *Lex Christi* principle. But what does it mean? The evangelical Christian is apt to boggle at the word "law", demanding, "What has the Gospel to do with law?" Nevertheless, as C. H. Dodd[1] has recently shown, Paul's use of the word "law" here is not accidental. Paul and his converts possessed a tradition of Christ's ethical

[1] See his essay *"Ennomos Christou"* in *Studia Paulina*.

teaching (Note how he quotes "commandments" of the Lord in I Cor. 7 and 9) which they regarded as an authoritative norm and pattern for the good life in much the same way as the Jew regarded the Torah. The Christian may be done with the law as a means of salvation, but, in Paul's view, he is *ennomos Christou* "under the law of Christ" (I Cor. 9.21): that is, under obligation to shape his conduct by the "design for life" given him in the Lord's teaching. And that is why, in Rom. 12–14, when Paul comes to set forth the ethical implications of his Gospel, he weaves into the fabric of his exhortation so many of the sayings of Jesus.

But "fulfilling the law of Christ" is a principle which Paul interpreted theologically as well as ethically. Several times, when he bids his converts imitate Christ and his ways, it is the Christ who came not from history—the supreme Moral Teacher—but from heaven—the divine Son of God —who is in his mind. Does he require the Corinthians to be generous? Then he reminds them of the Lord "who, though he was rich, for our sake became poor" (where the reference is clearly to the Incarnation). Does he desire the Philippians to be humble? Then he points them to him who, though he was divine by nature, laid his glory by to become a servant.

Such are some of the principles of Christian behaviour in St. Paul, none of them outmoded by the lapse of centuries. It remains to mention one more—*Agapē*. *Agapē*, a word notoriously difficult to translate—its best English equivalent is perhaps "caring"—is, for Paul, the very heart of Gospel goodness, because it is our human response to the divine love manifested in the sacrifice of Christ. (The Christian love ethic, it has been said, is the result of a love story— a love story in which the chief actor is not man but God.) Therefore, with unwearying insistence, he appeals for *Agapē*. "For love's sake I appeal to you", is his plea to Philemon for Onesimus. "If there be any incentive of love", he challenges the Philippians. "Be rooted and grounded in love", he writes in Ephesians. "Love is the greatest and most lasting thing there is", he tells the Corinthians.

"Love never fails." Here is something that time cannot touch or render obsolete, a law of life as valid for us as for Paul's converts. In our complicated modern world it will often not be easy to apply. "Love", Niebuhr[1] has said, "is always relevant but never a simple possibility." But it remains the supreme standard of Christian action. "When this is done, all is done."

[1] *Christian Faith and Social Action*, 12.

Chapter Five

THE HOPE OF GLORY

"Him that has aye something ayont, need never be weary", said the Fife labourer to Robert Louis Stevenson, when they talked together about the aims and ends of life. St. Paul would have concurred. Only he would never have left the "something ayont" so nebulous and undefined. For the Apostle, salvation as a future hope meant certain, very definite things. It was the very nerve of his Christianity, and without it a man might as well subscribe to the Epicurean philosophy of "Let us eat and drink, for tomorrow we die."

What this hope was, we may discover by studying such chapters in his letters as I Thess. 4, I Cor. 15, II Cor. 5 and Rom. 8. Its keywords are Resurrection, Parousia, Judgment, Glory, and it can be summed up in such sentences as these:

"Now is Christ risen from the dead and become the first-fruits of them that slept."

"Our commonwealth is in heaven, and from it we await a Saviour, the Lord Jesus Christ, who will change our lowly bodies to be like his glorious body."

"We must all appear before the judgment seat of Christ."

"I reckon that the sufferings of this present time are not worthy to be compared with the glory that is to be revealed to us."

No man may deny that such sentences fall strangely on

modern ears. Time was when our eschatologically minded forefathers dogmatized on such themes, and sometimes spoke as if all the secrets of God had been revealed to them. All this is changed. Men now profess their ignorance, and often their doubt. So deeply have the acids of contemporary scepticism corroded the faith of multitudes that for most the word "eschatology" means the question, "Do I live again after death?" (So we have books in plenty with titles like "Why I believe in personal Immortality" but few which faithfully reflect the New Testament teaching about the Last Things.) How incomparably grander in Paul's view was the eternal backcloth to the human drama! He thought cosmically, not merely in terms of individuals. He believed not simply in an after-life but in a final "wind-up" of human history, the coming of Christ in glory, the resurrection, the last judgment.

If the range of Paul's hope perplexes us, no less do its thought-forms. To minds taught to think in terms of progress and evolution, to say nothing of "the second law of thermodynamics", St. Paul's apocalyptic pictures of the ultimate destiny of man and the cosmos are strange and scandalous. Did I say cosmos? How utterly different is twentieth-century man's cosmology from the Apostle's! The "three-decker" conception of the universe held by the biblical writers—and by most men till the end of the Middle Ages—is shattered for ever. "The floor of heaven, inlaid with stars," as Froude put it, "has sunk back into an infinite abyss of immeasurable space; and the firm earth itself, unfixed from its foundations, is now seen to be but a small atom in the awful vastness of the universe."[1] All this has had its effect on man's thinking about the ultimate destiny of the race and has altered traditional views, drawn

[1] *History of England.*

from the Bible, about the Last Things. How can modern man be expected to take Paul as guide on the dark mysteries of his own and the world's future?

Nor has "the household of faith", however conservative it tends to be in its thinking, been untouched by this landslide in eschatology. The "fear o' Hell" is no more

> *a hangman's whip*
> *To haud the wretch in order,*

and it has been truthfully said that a Gallup poll in an ordinary congregation, or even in a theological college, on the question, "What do you believe about the Second Advent?" would be a shattering experiment.[1] Probably in no department of Christian theology so much as in eschatology does the gulf between us and the First Christians yawn so wide.

On the other hand, we have witnessed in this generation a notable revival in biblical theology, which has led us to rethink many of our cardinal doctrines. Christian theologians, long more deeply influenced than they knew by Greek views of time and eternity, are beginning to study again the biblical conceptions of these things. And it is growing clear that the time is ripe for a fresh approach to the whole subject of Christian eschatology. For one thing, as scholars from Schweitzer to Cullmann have been teaching us for the past few decades, the New Testament Gospel is radically eschatological. For a second point, a Christianity shorn of its eschatological hope has in more senses than one no future before it. And for a third, the history of our own times testifies that if religion does not furnish men with such a hope, they will very soon devise secular substitutes for it. (We think of Hitler's dream of a *Reich* which would last a

[1] John Robinson, *In the End—God*, 9.

thousand years; Mussolini's vision of a new and greater Roman Empire, and Marxism's myth of a class-less society after the final "show-down" between capitalism and communism.)

I do not doubt that if St. Paul were among us today he would attribute this landslide in eschatology to modern man's revolt from belief in the God of the Bible—the sovereign Lord of history, who was "in the beginning", who is even now working out his great purposes in time and who will be there "in the end" to complete his work. Paul, both as Jew and as Christian, believed in such a God, held such a view of the time-process, expected such an end to the travail of the ages. For him "the glittering tumult of history" mattered intensely: it was the scene of the redeeming acts of God; and the drama whose *peripeteia* had come with the coming of Christ was moving surely and steadily to its God-appointed close.

So it must be for us too. Unless the Church is prepared to scrap its Hebraic heritage and adopt a Greek *Weltanschauung* to which time is largely irrelevant, we also must look at the world and history and God as Paul does.

Does this mean that we must, as Christians, commit ourselves to a literal acceptance of all the details of Paul's teaching about the Last Things? No. We have to recognize that Paul's apocalyptic statements about the Last Things, taking as they do the form of myth and symbol (apocalyptic is mythologized eschatology) are "neither inerrant prophecies about the future nor pious guess-work".[1] We view them rightly as "transpositions into the key of the hereafter" of that sure knowledge of God which Paul had found in his encounter with the living Christ. Our task is to discover the basic truth embodied in Paul's myth or symbol

[1] John Robinson, *In the End—God*, 35.

—what is made sure to the heart by the witness of the Spirit —and to translate it into contemporary terms. Thus, for example, many of us may find it hard to accept the picture of the Parousia which Paul paints in the Thessalonian letters[1]; but we cannot, if we are to keep faith with the New Testament, reject the truth for which the symbol of the Second Advent stands.

With these prolegomena, we may now single out for discussion two or three of the main strands in St. Paul's Christian Hope.

I. THE BEGINNING OF THE END—"D-DAY IS PAST"

The first point to seize is that for Paul *the End had begun,* This is what we know nowadays as "realized eschatology". Though he makes but little use of "kingdom" phraseology, Paul shares with the rest of the apostolic writers the conviction that in the life, death and resurrection of Christ and the outpouring of the Spirit God's ancient promises to Israel have come true, the Reign of God has been decisively manifested, and the powers of the New Order—the Age to Come—set in motion. Christ has met and overcome "the last enemy", death; by his resurrection he has been declared to be the Son of God "with power"; and in his triumph all his People may share.

Cullmann has used the analogy of D-Day to express this apostolic conviction that "the strife is o'er, the battle won". It is the conviction that, though the campaign may drag on and V-Day—the day of the Final Victory—may still be out of sight, D-Day is over, and the powers of evil have received a blow from which they never can recover. In his

[1] "Painted in colours from the crudest palette of Jewish eschatology" (C. H. Dodd, *New Testament Studies*, 121).

Cross Christ has triumphed over them. Now, raised from the dead, he dies no more, for he lives for ever by the power of God.

I do not think this note is sufficiently heard in our worship today. Once a year, on Easter morning, we hear it struck as it should be. But do we realize that every Christian congregation ought to be a Community of the Resurrection, as every Sunday ought to be an Easter festival? Do we not rather tend to sing for the rest of the year hymns with the theme:

Thy kingdom come, O God
Thy rule, O Christ, begin.

Such sentiments, born of a sad awareness of the evil still remaining in the world, we may respect and even sympathize with, in certain moods; but they fail to reproduce the authentic New Testament conviction that Christians have already been "translated out of the kingdom of darkness into the kingdom of his dear Son". They fail to testify that we are living in a world in which, for all its sin and sadness, Christ has left one vacant tomb in the wide graveyard of the earth, and that his victory is like the breach in a North Sea dyke, an event of apparently small importance whose consequences are incalculable—

"Beyond the dyke is the tumultuous sea, which will burst through the opening—so Paul knew, when he had met the Risen One, that he is the first-born of them that slept."[1]

But there is more to it than this. Paul and his fellow-Apostles were sure not only that Christ was risen but that he was now reigning. Two words summed up the earliest Christian confession of faith—*Kyrios Jesus*, "Jesus is Lord"; and when the first Christians uttered them, they were not

---

[1] Karl Heim (quoted by J. S. Stewart in *A Faith to Proclaim*, 134).

merely conferring on Jesus an honorific title; they were affirming, with the full force of their hearts and minds, that Jesus was *now ruling* over God's People and God's world. If the world with all its evil still went on, if Christ's was a hidden kingship, one day the veils would be swept away.

Christus regnat![1] These are the very accents of Pauline, of apostolic, Christianity. If we have tended to forget them, the Church in the times of her greatest crises has always had them on her lips. Our forefathers were not slow to proclaim the "crown rights of the Redeemer" in face of all who menaced them. In the days before and during the last war the persecuted Christians of Europe, as Visser 't Hooft[2] has told us, rose to a revivified belief in the kingship of Christ. It is an article in our *Credo*, which we must ever seek to reaffirm. We must believe not only in a risen but also in a regnant Christ.

2. THE HOPE OF THE DAY OF CHRIST

But Paul's gospel, like that of the whole New Testament, was set in a framework of both realized and futurist eschatology. D-Day was but the prelude to V-Day—the Day of Christ, the *Parousia*, the day of the final victory of God in Christ. For Paul's hope was nothing if not cosmic in its scope. (Here is one obvious point of difference between St.

[1] Dr. John Brown, author of *Rab and his Friends*, tells how he once heard his revered father, Dr. Brown of Broughton Place, Edinburgh, preaching on the second psalm, "Why do the heathen rage?" Pushing up his spectacles and aside his papers, Dr. Brown cried to the congregation, "Where is Jesus now? And where are those priests and rulers now? Jesus is gone up, and has sat down, and shall forever sit, on the throne of the universe. Where they are, in heaven or in hell, I know not; but this I do know that wherever they may be, they are, and forever shall be, *at*, or *under*, his feet." *Letters of Dr. John Brown*, 86.   [2] *The Kingship of Christ.*

Paul and modern Christianity. Whereas we think of Christ's saving work as securing the means whereby individuals may pass at death into Paradise, Paul looked forward to a cosmic consummation and a coming of Christ in glory.) Dr. Eric Rust[1] has well described the relation between the D-Day and the V-Day of the New Testament:

"The *eschaton*, the end of history, has already come in Jesus Christ and time has already been filled with eternity, yet the very hiddenness of the *eschaton* implies that this period of hiddenness must end in a final consummation when the full glory shall shine forth. *Then*, what is happening in the present period of history, when the *aeons* overlap and the powers of the coming *aeon* are at work in historical time, will be summed up and made plain. *Then*, the judgment that is already supervening upon men and the salvation that is already effective in their lives will be gathered up into a fully consummated eternal order, and history will be no more. *Then*, the Christ, whose glory is known only to faith, will stand forth in his supernal splendour, and the mists of history will be taken up into the unbounded and unfettered eternity of God."

If then we are to retain any sort of vital connexion with Paul's Gospel, how ought we to think of the Coming of Christ?

St. Paul and many of the early Christians, as everybody knows, believed the Parousia, or "royal visit", of Christ to be very near (though the belief in its imminence does not bulk nearly so large in his later letters as it does in the two Epistles to Thessalonica). The event has proved them mistaken. The *Parousia* in that sense has not yet taken place. But the man who wrote the Second Epistle of Peter, reflecting on this, made the wise suggestion that time measurements hardly applied to this Event: "With the Lord," he

[1] *Theology Today*, Oct., 1953, 349.

said, "one day is as a thousand years, and a thousand years as one day". Moreover, certain sayings of our Lord about "the Day of the Son of man" suggest that the early Christians were wrong in trying to fix any kind of date, because the coming of the Son of man lies outside our time-reckoning altogether—is, in fact, dateless.[1] Does this mean that the symbol of the Second Advent is of no concern or importance to us?

This would be a very rash and wrong conclusion. "The symbol of the second coming of Christ", Reinhold Niebuhr[2] has written, "can neither be taken literally nor dismissed as unimportant." Why? Take it literally—locate it in the time-series—and you make the ultimate vindication of God *over* history (which is what the consummation of the kingdom of God means) into a mere point *in* history. Treat it, on the other hand, as unimportant, and you get a view of eternity which annuls, not fulfils, the process of history.

If, then, we are to take the New Testament symbol of the Second Advent seriously, then I suggest that we must say three things about it.

First, the doctrine of the Second Coming expresses the certitude of Christian faith that the Lord of history, who is the Father of Christ, will complete his saving work. "Belief in eschatology", says Lesslie Newbigin,[3] "without belief in a real End is like belief in religion without belief in God." Here we may consider the concept of the Last Judgment. No one can read Paul's letters without seeing how basic this doctrine was to him, and how he lets the awe of it descend upon his heart to keep his conscience quick. Nor can we today jettison the truth for which the concept stands, viz.

[1] See C. H. Dodd, *The Coming of Christ*, 7.
[2] *The Nature and Destiny of Man*, II, 299.
[3] *The Reunion of the Church*, 74.

that when men and their deeds finally come face to face with God, the difference between good and evil cannot be swallowed up in "a distinctionless eternity". We may not, like our forefathers, think of "legal proceedings on a gigantic scale" at the chronological end of history. We know that judgment is going on now and always. Yet however inconceivable the idea may be to our minds, the faith we hold in a righteous God and the ethical view we take of the world and history compel us to believe that God must finally vindicate himself as the moral governor of the world, finalize his verdicts and reward men according to the good and the evil they have done.

In the second place, we should think of the coming of Christ not as an event in history but as the point at which (in C. H. Dodd's phrase) the race reaches its last frontier-post and encounters—not nothingness but God in Christ: the point at which our time—that is, human history with all its values acceptable to him—will be taken up into God's eternity.

And, thirdly, our clue to the nature of the Second Coming is Christ's First Coming. God has already revealed himself to us in a Man by whom all may know what sort of Person it is with whom, at the end of history, we have to do. When the scroll of history is wound up, there will be nothing contrary to what Christ disclosed at his first advent. We shall encounter the same Person whose holiness, truth and love we already know in Christ; and if we have to "appear before the judgment seat of Christ", we may believe that the sign of the Cross will be over all.

3. THE YEARS OF GRACE

D-Day is past; V-Day is to come; and Christians meanwhile live their lives in the faith that the God who has inaugurated the New Age will yet consummate it in glory. Such was Paul's view. But what of the time between the mid-point of history and its end, "the years of grace" as they are often called? Did Paul regard this *interim* as simply a period of ding-dong warfare between the forces of good and evil? Or did he see these years of grace as ordained by God for the working out of some positive pattern and purpose?

This is a question of much importance for us, especially in these days when the secular hope, viz. the belief in inevitable and automatic progress, has been sadly shattered by the recent course of world events. A century ago, and even more recently, when the belief in progress was at its zenith Christians, in tune with the *Zeitgeist*, were wont to sing fervently:

> *Jesus shall reign where'er the sun*
> *Does his successive journeys run.*

Nowadays the hope of a world at the feet of Christ does not burn so brightly, and not a few Christians, transferring their hope completely to the heavenly world, have abandoned Isaac Watts's optimism. Has Paul any guidance for us here? We do him wrong if we simply summarize his view as "The time is shortened". Because Paul held that the day of Christ was not far distant, we too easily forget that he believed the years of grace had a purpose and would last long enough for its fulfilment. That purpose was the evangelization of the world. He sees the years of grace as the time for a Christian mission which would culminate in the conversion not only of the Gentiles but of his unbelieving fellow-countrymen (Rom. 11.28–32). Believing that God's purpose is to "sum up all things in Christ" (Eph. 1.10), he conceives of Christ as exercising his sovereignty till all hostile powers are subdued (I Cor. 15.25).

Clearly Paul does not share modern pessimism about the

cause of Christ in history; rather, he foresees a triumphal "progress in Christ" diffusing the knowledge of God in every place (II Cor. 2.14). *Vexilla Regis prodeunt*, and Paul expects them to advance a great way further before the End.

What may we learn from this? Surely that St. Paul—and he does not stand alone in the New Testament—gives no support to Christians who take a defeatist view about the future of earthly history. We have apostolic warrant for regarding the years of grace as a God-given time for carrying the Gospel to all creation, and for believing that the Christ who now lives and reigns in grace will spread his conquests wider and yet wider before the End comes. If the New Testament gives no warrant for the nineteenth-century conviction that human civilization is marching irresistibly to perfection, it does authorize us to hope that, in the words of the Scottish paraphrase,

> *The beam that shines from Sion hill*
> *Shall lighten every land,*

and to go forward to our missionary task in the persuasion that God wills that human society, while the world lasts, shall be more and more conformed to the mind of Christ. This is the Christian optimism which informs Principal John Baillie's book *The Belief in Progress*, an optimism too little represented in the Christian tradition, but to which we are now recalled. "We must recover", he says,[1] "that sense of standing on the threshold of a new historical dispensation, that sense of a noble prospect opening out before us, that sense of the power of the Spirit and of the inexhaustible resources now available to us, that adventurous zeal for the renewal of humanity, and that confidence in ultimate victory of which the New Testament is so full."

[1] Op. cit., 220.

4. THE HEART OF THE CHRISTIAN HOPE

"It is unwise", writes Niebuhr,[1] "for Christians to claim any knowledge of either the furniture of heaven or the temperature of hell; or to be too certain about any details of the kingdom of God in which history is consummated." We may heed this warning, acknowledging its justice, while yet believing that St. Paul can teach us something about the heart of the Christian hope.

Let us first make two simple points.

In the first place, as "God alone hath immortality", immortal life for St. Paul, as for all the New Testament writers, is the gift of God in Christ. We are not immortal beings in our own right, so to speak. Just as St. John says, "He that hath the Son hath life", so Paul holds that our hope of immortality is bound up with belonging to Christ—with "Christ in us, the hope of glory". "Only *one* life", says Denney,[2] "has ever won the victory over death: only one life ever can win it—the kind which was in him, which *is* in him, which he shares with all those whom faith makes one with him. That is our hope, to be really members of Christ, living with a life which comes from God and has already vanquished death."

The second point is this. Plato's hope was set on the immortality of the soul. Paul's is set on the resurrection of the body—"the spiritual body", as he explains in I Cor. 15, for manifestly our present frame of flesh and blood is doomed to dissolution. *Sōma*, "body", as Paul uses it, has its nearest English equivalent in the word "personality". It is not as disembodied souls but as whole men, Paul would teach us, that we shall live hereafter. But this "body", this "frame"—call it what you will—will be marvellously transformed in the world to come.

[1] Op cit., 304.   [2] *The Way Everlasting*, 188.

It follows from all this that what is important is not the moment of bodily death but the time when a man comes to be "in Christ". (I do not find that Paul has much to say about the destiny of those who never knew, or have rejected Christ; but despite the "larger hope" of Rom. 11—"God has consigned all men to disobedience that he may have mercy upon all"—I am pretty sure that the Apostle was not a "universalist" in our modern sense.) The life hereafter will therefore not be a new life but rather the life which a man "in Christ" already has, only lived under new and unimaginably glorious conditions:

> "What no eye has seen, nor ear heard
> Nor the heart of man conceived,
> What God has prepared for those who love him"
> (I Cor. 2.9).

The relationship of "in Christ" will have given place to that of being "with Christ", and our "lowly bodies" will have become like his "glorious" body.

Likewise, Paul may teach us two things about the state of the saints in glory. It will be at once corporate and Christ-like. How pregnant with suggestion is Rom. 8.29: "For those whom he foreknew he also predestined to be conformed to the image of his Son, that he might be the first-born among many brethren." Paul thinks of the life hereafter as a family life—a life of fellowship with God and with one another in the Body of Christ, which dwells partly in this life and partly in the other:

> *One family we dwell in him*
> *One Church above, beneath.*

The consummation of the Christian hope is a great society of redeemed persons living for ever with their Lord in a fellowship no longer hampered by the flesh, no longer exposed to the assaults of sin, no longer at the mercy of death; for "this corruptible will have put on incorruption", and Christ's men and women will be "at home" with their Lord in a beatitude which eye hath not seen, nor ear heard, nor heart conceived. Then they will see no longer "in a mirror dimly" but "face to face".

"Conformed to the image of his Son"—this, ethically and spiritually, is the Christian destiny. "Every Christian", says C. S. Lewis,[1] "is to become a little Christ. The whole purpose of becoming a Christian is simply that, nothing else." Men have painted many pictures of the heavenly state —unending sensual bliss, absorption into the All, Nirvana and the like. Paul holds fast to what is essential. "We shall be like him." Salvation, full and final, is sharing the likeness of Christ, who is God's true image—and Christ we know.

To such a hope Paul bids us lift our hearts. With such a hope in view he enjoins us to "labour in the Lord" unwearyingly. This hope does not disappoint us, because through the Spirit, which is the "arles" of our future inheritance, we already know in our hearts the love of God. Communist gibes about "pie in the sky when you die" should not worry us unduly. They would not have worried Paul. For him the heavenly hope was no "grand perhaps" but "a solid weight of glory"; no opiate of the people but a spiritual inheritance to challenge us to make our calling and election sure; a hope so great and so divine as to beget in us "immortal longings" and to give human life a meaning and an end which the men of our day, groping about in darkness and despair, need more than anything else to make them feel that life is worth living, that Christ is God's clue to its meaning, and that "the best is yet to be".

[1] *Beyond Personality*, 28.

Note on St. Paul and Predestination

Election and Predestination are two cognate Pauline doctrines not now much in vogue. The average man today, if he believes in God, generally doubts whether God has an eternal plan for men and nations. Election suggests to him Calvinism, the Westminster Confession of Faith and doctrines of divine sovereignty now, as he supposes, deservedly discredited. If he is a Scot, he has read "Holy Willie's Prayer" with its merciless indictment of eighteenth-century Calvinistic conceptions of Election, and he has a vague suspicion that this "ferocious theology" with its God who sends

Ane to Heaven an' ten to Hell

all for his glory, goes back behind Calvin and Augustine to the Apostle Paul. What truth is there in this?

St. Paul most certainly believed in Election and Predestination. Two brief passages from his letters make this pellucidly clear:

"He chose us in him (Christ) before the foundation of the world, that we should be holy and blameless before him. He destined us in love to be his sons through Jesus Christ, according to the purpose of his will" (Eph. 1.4f.).

"For those whom he foreknew he also predestined to be conformed to the image of his Son, in order that he might be the first among many brethren. And those whom he predestined he also called; and those whom he called he also justified; and those whom he justified he also glorified" (Rom. 8.29f.).

The man who wrote these words believed not only that God was the supreme Disposer of all things but that he elected from eternity to save some men and predestined them to glory. Is this an absurd and ridiculous belief? Is it not, basically, the conviction that we just do not happen to exist—that our life has its roots in eternity—and that our salvation (if we are conscious of such a thing) begins in the eternal God (as the work of art begins first in the mind of the artist), and is actualized in Christ, the divinely sent Saviour of men?

But does not Paul go further than this? Indeed, he does in Rom. 9.17–21, a passage which every lover of St. Paul must wish he had never written. Here the problem before him is the Jews' failure to accept Christ and the Gospel, and inevitably he has to discuss the place of free will in the divine purpose. His argument is that since God is sovereign, he can do as he wills, even with his own chosen People. Unfortunately he so over-drives the argument as to conclude: "God has mercy upon whomever he wills, and he hardens the heart of whomever he wills." Were this true, God would come near being a non-moral despot, like Hardy's "President of the Immortals." And, alas, Paul does not improve matters by producing in the next verses his analogy of the Potter and the clay, in order to silence all cavillers. But, in fairness to the Apostle, we must add that, if in Rom. 9 Paul says God can make his People "vessels of wrath", he goes on to say in Rom. 11 that these same vessels of wrath will finally be saved!

The truth is that Paul's doctrine of election "crops up as a pure expression of the religious experience of grace." Says Rudolf Otto[1]:

"A man who is the object of grace, when he looks back on himself, feels more and more that he has become what he is by no act or activity of his own, that grace came to him without his own will or power, that it took hold of him, drove him, led him on. Before any act of his own, he sees redeeming love seeking and choosing him, and recognizes an eternal decree of grace on his behalf."

[1] *Das Heilige* (Dodd's translation), 109.

This is Paul's experience, and the experience of many since who have known God's grace. The stress is thrown wholly on the divine initiative of grace in election. But does not Paul also lay great weight on the importance of the human response? Of course he does. To return for a moment to Rom. 9–11, we note that if in chapter 9 he implies that God has rejected the Jews, in chapter 10 he argues that they have really by their unbelief rejected themselves. In all this he is grappling with the ancient problem of the relation of divine sovereignty to human free will, a problem which, since we lack omniscience, is ultimately as mysterious as the existence of evil in a world made by a good God. Yet, little as we understand this mystery, our best wisdom is to hold *both* convictions, viz. that our salvation is grounded in the eternal will of God, and that such salvation depends upon a man's own response to the grace of God offered him in Christ.

Now let us consider predestination more closely. Did Paul really teach the pernicious doctrine of "Double Predestination", namely, that God has from all eternity willed that some should be saved, and that some should be reprobated for ever?

The short answer is No. Reprobation is "the shadow side" of the doctrine of election. But into that shadow side Paul does not peer. Not a word does he say about men being predestinated by God to eternal damnation. It is true that to say that some people are eternally elected to salvation implies, in logic, that others are eternally rejected. In logic, yes; but Paul is here splendidly illogical. What Paul does say is this. The Gospel comes to all men, challenging them to the decision of faith. All hangs on that decision. If Paul speaks of "perishing" (as he does), it is never of something which simply is. The possibility of it is mentioned in order to evoke faith. He says in effect, "If you perish, it is your own fault. If you have saving faith, then know it is a gift of God's grace." The opposite of election, for the Apostle, is not predestination to perdition: it is unbelief— a self-incurred thing. And if we draw the logical conclusion of election, as the Calvinists undoubtedly did, then we clash with the sovereign truth of the Bible that God gave Christ in order that men might not perish but have eternal life. No man may hold that God has eternally predestined even one soul to damnation and still hold that God is love.

What Paul says—and we must say too—is this: If God wills to save you who are a sinner, that is his pure grace. That he does so will, he tells you in Christ. If you refuse God's offer, you run the risk of perishing.

INDEX

SUBJECTS

Adam and Eve, 71, 77
Adoption, 18, 36
Agapē, 47f., 57, 108, 119f.
Atonement, 29ff., 81, 88ff.

Baptism, 34f., 37, 105
Body, the spiritual, 54f., 133

Christ, conception of, in Paul,
  56–63
—, the cosmic, 60f., 103
—, the imitation of, 46f., 119
—, the kingship of, 127
—, the living, 59, 82f., 96f.
—, the titles of, 61f.
Christianity, pre-Pauline, 18f.
Church, doctrine of, 41f., 99f.
—, as Body of Christ, 42f., 103
—, as institution, 101
Communication, problem of, 85
Conversion, Paul's, 19f.
Corporate personality, 38, 43

"D-Day", 52, 125
Demonic, belief in, 74f.

Ecclēsia, 42
Election, Paul's doctrine of, 136–
  139
Eschatology, Paul's, 50ff., 121ff.
Ethics, Pauline, 45f., 114ff.

Faith, 24f., 32ff., 71
Fellowship with Christ, 21, 37,
  53, 94ff., 134f.
Flesh, 24f., 71

Gospel, definition of Paul's, 13

Hellenism, 17f.
Hilastērion, 30f.
Hope, the Christian, 50ff., 121ff.
Household Rules, 48

"In Christ", 37f., 95ff., 99ff.

Jesus, Paul's knowledge of
  historic, 56f.
Judaism, 17
Judgment, 53, 129f.
Justification by faith, 21, 26f.,
  86f.

Kērygma, 18, 56, 88
Koinōnia, 45, 104, 118

Law, 25f., 46, 69f., 135
Lex Christi, 97, 118f.
Life (salvation), 37, 94
Lord, Jesus as, 61f., 126f.

Marriage, Paul's view of, 49
Messiah, Jesus the, 61
Mission, the Church's, 44, 103
Mystery religions, 18, 104
Mysticism, Pauline, 38, 98

Paraenesis, 116
Parousia, 50, 52, 123, 127ff.
Penal substitution, 32, 91f.
Predestination, 136ff.
Prodigal Son, parable of, 28, 87f.
Progress, belief in, 73, 131f.

Reconciliation, 28f., 87f.
Redemption, 23, 86
Reprobation, 138f.
Resurrection, 32, 96f., 126
Reunion of Church, 102, 111
Righteousness of God, 27

Sacraments, Paul's view of, 44f.,
   104ff.
Salvation, 21f., 94, and *passim*
Sanctification, 36, 94f.
Second Advent; see *Parousia*
Sin, Paul's view of, 23f., 68ff.
Slavery, 49
Sōma, 54, 113
Son of God, Jesus as the, 62

Spirit, the Holy, 39f., 46, 82,
   107ff.
State, Paul's attitude to, 49
Stoicism, 18
Supper, the Lord's, 44f., 105f.

"Universalism", Paul's, 54, 131,
   134

"V-Day", 52, 127f.

Words of the Lord, 19, 118f.
"Works", salvation by, 15, 25,
   83, 115
Wrath of God, 69f., 79f., 88

"Years of grace", 130ff.

AUTHORS

Abelard, 90
Anselm, 76
Asquith, 69
Aulén, 90f.

Baillie, J., 57, 132
Barth, 14, 25, 67f.
Berdyaev, 79
Brooks, 98
Brown, Dr. John, 127
Browning, 55, 68
Brunner, 28, 50, 77, 88, 100, 113f.
Bultmann, 99
Bunyan, 36, 84
Burns, 123, 136

Cairns, D. S., 14, 106
Calvin, 38
Chalmers, 84
Craig, 105
Cullmann, 34, 52, 91, 125

Dahl, 61
Davies, 104
Deissmann, 21, 39, 56
Denney, 13, 58, 67, 71, 84, 89, 133
Dodd, 49, 118, 125, 130
Drinkwater, 97
Duncan, 38

Filson, 38
Flemington, 34
Fox, 114
Frederick, 68
Froude, 122

George, 96

Hegel, 73
Heim, 126
Hume, 112

Inge. 101

Jefferies, 30
Joad, 74
Jowett. 89

Lewis, 135
Lightfoot, Bp., 22
Lindsay, Sir David, 13
Luther, 14, 21, 33, 76, 80, 91, 95

Mackay, 100
Manson, T. W., 44
Maurice, 111f.
Moody, Campbell, 83
Murray, G., 17

Newbigin, 129
Niebuhr, 71, 73, 120, 129, 133
Nygren, 32, 95

Oman, 18
Otto, 137

Palmer, 98

Read, 85
Renan, 13
Robinson, H. Wheeler, 35, 113
Robinson, J. A. T., 124

Rossetti, 113
Rust, 128

Schweitzer, 95
Shaw, 76
Stevenson, 121
Stewart, 55, 76, 91, 96

Talbot, 74
Taylor, V., 26, 86
Thompson, 98

Vidler, 58, 112
Visser 't Hooft, 99, 127

Waddell, Helen, 90
Watts, 131
Webb, Mary, 70
Weinel, 21, 115
Whitman, 73
Whittier, 98
Whyte, 77
Winer, 91